Successful Reservoir Fly Fishing Techniques

A Trout Angler's Guide to Improved Catches

Successful Reservoir Fly Fishing Techniques

A Trout Angler's Guide to Improved Catches

Adrian V. W. Freer

THE CROWOOD PRESS

First published in 2007 by
The Crowood Press Ltd
Ramsbury, Marlborough
Wiltshire SN8 2HR

www.crowood.com

British Library Cataloguing-in-Publication Data
A catalogue record for this book is available from the British Library.

ISBN 987 1 86126 930 0

Dedication
To my wife Louise, who puts up with my fly fishing fanaticism with great patience and forbearance, and who still encourages me to go fishing when things are getting on top of me. She also gave me encouragement while I was writing this book. An understanding wife is one of the greatest assets any fly fisherman can have, and I consider myself very fortunate to be so blessed.

Disclaimer
The author and the publisher do not accept any responsibility in any manner whatsoever for any error or omission, nor any loss, damage, injury or liability of any kind incurred as a result of the use of any of the information contained in this book, or reliance upon it.

Frontispiece
The author with a 7lb 8oz rainbow trout from Elinor Trout Fishery in Northamptonshire. It was taken on a size 12 Black & Red Holographic Buzzer and took 22min to land.

Typeset in Plantin by Bookcraft Ltd, Stroud, Gloucestershire

Printed and bound in Singapore by Craft Print International Ltd

Contents

Acknowledgements   6
Introduction   7

 1 Why Do We Go Trout Fishing?   10
 2 Tackle: Rods and Fly Lines   14
 3 Tackle: Reels and Accessories   25
 4 Casting and the Necessity for Distance   34
 5 Terminal Tackle, Leader Materials and Knots   41
 6 A Reasoned Approach to Fly Choice   52
 7 Leader Construction, Retrieve Methods and the 'Take'   62
 8 On the Bank: An Enquiring Mind and Some Important Questions   77
 9 Valuable Information Straight from the Fish's Mouth   88
10 The Food of Reservoir Trout: Quantity and Frequency   100
11 Tactics   112
12 Bank Fishing and Boat Fishing   128
13 Fly Dressing: Good Reasons for Tying Your Own Flies   141
14 Recommended Fly Patterns   148
15 The Weather, Water Conditions and Seasons,
    and their Influence on the Fish   164
16 On the Future of Fly Fishing   174

Postscript   180
Appendix I: Supplementary List of Fly Patterns   185
Appendix II: Construction Details of Tackle Accessories   186
Appendix III: Fishing Record Card   188
Bibliography   189
Index   190

Acknowledgements

I would like to express my thanks to all those anglers who have helped me, over the years, in my angling pilgrimage, firstly as a coarse angler and latterly as a fly fisherman.

Firstly, to the memory of my late grandfather, Robert H.M. Freer, who took me under his wing at a very early age and taught me initially to catch roach and gudgeon from the Leicester Canal in the early 1950s. Then, after I was well and truly hooked, he taught me to catch perch, tench, carp and bream as well.

Secondly, my thanks go to all those who have advised and encouraged me, and thankfully still do, as I endeavour to progress and improve my skills and catch rates. Many of them are anglers who I have met on the bank and are unknown to me by name, but nevertheless they have helped me greatly. Those I can name include Mal Wright, the finest fly tyer I know, Graham Herbert, match fisherman par excellence, Andy Miller, the fishery manager at Eyebrook Reservoir, and Ifor Jones, the manager at Thornton Reservoir. Their words of wisdom have been more valuable than they probably realize.

Thirdly, I extend my thanks to all the members of the Leicestershire Fly Fishing Association (the LFFA) who are a great bunch of anglers. They possess great fishing skills and are enormous fun at our monthly meetings and on the bank on club days.

Fourthly, I have to mention three fishermen who helped me in my coarse fishing career and who taught me to think problems through rather than using set methods without any thought: David Ward, the late Ivan Marks (probably the greatest British match angler who has ever lived) and Roy Marlow. Their help was invaluable, and the disciplines learnt from them helped me when I transferred to fly fishing.

Lastly, what can be said about the trout that hasn't been said before? Such a fine and cunning adversary; worth all the time and effort we anglers put into the sport. Some I have caught, others have utterly defeated me, but my respect for such a sleek, beautiful, powerful, intelligent, courageous, cunning, tenacious and, on occasion, very frustrating and capricious quarry knows no bounds.

Introduction

It is a good idea for the author of every book to explain why it was written, and as this book will be concerned to a great extent with asking relevant questions and then endeavouring to find the correct answers to them, perhaps the best way of explanation is to look at the who, the what, the how and the why.

Firstly, for whom has this book been written? It is aimed primarily at the improving trout angler who has been fly fishing for a couple of seasons, caught a few fish and who wishes to progress further; although it is hoped that all anglers, however experienced they are, will find something to interest, stimulate or inspire them.

Secondly, what is it about? It is about developing an enquiring mind, and acquiring those fishing skills and techniques that will enable him or her to perform more consistently.

Thirdly, and most importantly, how do we achieve all this? The following factors are important: having the right equipment, asking and then answering the right questions, building up an armoury of fishing methods that will cover most eventualities, being able and willing to be flexible and experiment as the need arises, having an eye for detail and a desire for perfection, and having the persistence to carry on in adverse conditions and not give up in spite of the lack of apparent results, until success has finally been achieved.

Finally, why fly fishing? If the reader has already started fly fishing then the answer will be crystal clear; if he has not then read Chapter 1 for a few more suggestions. But be warned, it is a sport that is as addictive as it is fascinating.

The results of catches over a season from most reservoirs show that the average catch is around three fish, per rod, per day. For the beginner to reach this average may seem like a distant dream, but it is certainly not beyond the reach of most ordinary anglers providing they are prepared to put some effort into their endeavours. To improve beyond that level is well within reach after three or four seasons. The author would sincerely hope that following the guidance given in this book will help the reader to improve their catch rate in a short time, hopefully interspersed with a few limit bags and the occasional large fish, with the minimum of blanks. Once that stage has been reached, the reader will have become a thinking angler – and will no longer need this book.

We all get blanks, sometimes when the conditions are dreadful, which we can expect, but also on those occasions when we are full of expectation, which dents our confidence. It is the skill and dogged persistence that enables some fly anglers to winkle the odd trout out when others are struggling that sorts out the above-average angler from the merely run-of-the-mill performer.

What qualifications, you may ask, does the author have to put pen to paper and give his advice on the subject? It is simply

A limit bag of rainbows from Eyebrook Reservoir. With good weather, beautiful surroundings and some fine fish into the bargain, what more could anyone ask?

that he too has been on the receiving end of a great deal of helpful advice and encouragement in his early (and later!) fishing career from many obliging and experienced anglers. It is his desire to make as much of this knowledge as possible, as well as the results of his own experiments and experiences, available to others who may well be going through this same learning curve.

Adopt, Adapt, Modify or Dismiss

No two anglers are alike in their physique, technique, patience or temperament, and all through this book it will be emphasized that, in order to progress in the sport, the angler should never follow any methods and techniques blindly, however successful they may appear to be. Rather, they should adopt those that prove to be successful for them and fit into their angling philosophy, adapt those that are not entirely right for them, modify those that do not work well, and dismiss those that do not deliver the goods at all. The results of adopting this approach will be interspersed through the pages which follow.

It may be surprising, but it is nevertheless true, that what works for one angler does not necessarily work for another, and only by being critical, discerning and willing to experiment will improvement ever be made and a lot of wasted time avoided. At the outset of his fly fishing career the author endeavoured to implement this philosophy, and it is strongly recommended that the reader do the same.

So Much to Learn

Fly fishing for reservoir trout has one thing in common with every other complex subject – the more one learns about it, the more one comes to realize how little one actually knows and how much more there is still to be discovered. It is all too easy to make assumptions and deductions that are based on what would logically be expected, but trout can often be extremely illogical, at least to the human mind, and understanding them only comes with time and experience.

In reality, trout are unreasoning creatures that are driven by their natural instincts to feed, to avoid predators and to reproduce their own kind, and they are wary, resourceful, they learn from their experiences to some degree, and they possess very acute natural senses that can test our angling skills (and patience) to the limit. That being the case, it is necessary to try and gain as much insight as possible into how the fish behave, about their environment, and how the conditions affect them if we are to deceive them.

Learning to be a successful fly angler is not easy, and it takes time and effort, but it is ultimately worthwhile when a shimmering rainbow trout has been deceived into taking, has been successfully played and netted, and eventually lies on the bank. It may take a lifetime of study to become a successful trout angler, but there is something gratifying in always being able to learn something new.

Although there is a great comradeship among fly fishers, it is nevertheless a lone sport in many ways, and especially so for the beginner who starts out on his own and who can be so easily daunted when he is not having success and has no one to turn to for advice. That is one of the reasons why joining a club can be of great benefit, as many experienced anglers are thankfully more than willing to pass on the benefit of their accumulated wisdom. It is sad, but true, that some fly anglers are secretive about their flies and methods, and we must be grateful to those who *are* willing to help their less knowledgeable brother and sister anglers.

It is the author's sincere desire that by adopting the disciplines and techniques outlined here, the reader will achieve a greater measure of success and satisfaction in his or her angling career. Like many participant sports today, fly fishing is in decline and sadly novices are not coming into the ranks as quickly as the older generation are passing away. If this book can do something to reverse that trend it will be an added bonus.

Tight lines and screaming reels to you all, and may your tying thread never break!

Adrian V.W. Freer

1 Why Do We Go Trout Fishing?

The author believes that the answer is simple: it is because fly fishing is the greatest sport known to mankind! A sweeping statement to make perhaps, and one with which anyone who is not a fly angler would probably disagree, but it is one that the author sincerely and passionately believes to be true.

'Passionate' is probably the defining word, because unless one is wholehearted in any leisure pursuit, or indeed in anything else that we turn our hands to, then nothing will truly grip us. True and deep satisfaction comes from taking time, effort and thinking problems through, and we only take out as much as we put in. Trout fishing is a sport that enables us to be enthusiastic in what we do. It is a sport that enables us to stretch ourselves to our extremes mentally, physically and also, dare I say, spiritually and so discover who we really are and what our limits are.

But how can such a statement – that fly fishing for trout is the greatest sport – be justified? What makes fishing for the humble trout with rod, fly line and artificial fly such a rewarding exercise? It is a sport that causes grown men to spend hours on the water endeavouring to deceive a trout, and the hours when they are off the water designing flies and developing tackle to aid them to do so. And, let us face it,

A fine hen rainbow trout of 5lb 5oz and one of 1lb 12oz. Both were caught on a Black & Green Marabou fished on a slow sinking line.

when they are doing neither of the above, and when they should perhaps be thinking about other things, their minds wander back again and again to simply contemplating their sport, reliving their successes, bemoaning their failures, and then thinking up new and better ways of improving their chances next time.

Reasons Why We Fly Fish for Trout

There are many reasons why fly fishing is the great sport it is, but let us consider a few justifications for that bold assertion.

Firstly, fly fishing usually takes place in the countryside and, for those of us who are city dwellers, the excuse for being in the countryside, to be alone and quiet with nature and our quarry is a pleasure in and of itself, long before our fly rod is taken out of its tube.

Then there is the trout itself. When God created the trout, whether it be a rainbow or a brownie, He must have taken great delight in His handiwork. There is surely no more breathtaking sight to behold than a trout that has just been landed, with its gleaming and speckled beauty, its perfectly proportioned elegance, and its implicit, latent power.

Fly fishing makes us think things out for ourselves, and that is a positive aspect. I do not subscribe to the fallacy that when we are involved in any 'leisure' pursuit we should automatically put our brains out of gear. It takes both thought *and* skill to deceive the fish, and that is why I think that catching a hard fighting trout, one that has taxed our brains and reasoning to the limit, must be eminently more rewarding than throwing three consecutive darts in treble twenty, however much skill that might involve.

There is something about the mechanics of casting with a fly rod that is like no other. When the fly is correctly delivered with the precision and delicacy for which we strive, it is akin to an art form in itself. Nothing in this world that is worthwhile is ever attained without effort, practice and application, and learning to cast with a fly rod is no different. It may take time and patience, but a well-executed, long and accurate cast, when the fly lands where and how the angler wants it to, is worth all the tears and frustration that learning entails.

Fly fishing allows us to satisfy that subconscious hunter–gatherer instinct present in us all. No matter how much modern man progresses, this indefinable and inborn characteristic can never be entirely suppressed by so-called civilized man in his so-called civilized environment. Could it be something to do with the build up and subsequent release of adrenaline, which can only be genuinely satisfied by the deception and capture of a wild quarry like the trout? We do not really know, but our sport more than fulfils and satisfies that deep need present within us.

Fly dressing is an art, so much so that the beautiful creations of fur and feather that we produce are often used to adorn the walls of those who have no interest in our sport whatsoever. How much more satisfying then is the creation of an artificial fly, preferably one that has been designed as well as tied by us, which deceives our unsuspecting quarry into believing that it is something edible and something that it should take into its mouth.

The manufacture and modification of fishing tackle, whether it be as substantial as making a split cane fishing rod from scratch, or simply tying up a nylon leader, may be rather more mundane, but it does allow us the satisfaction of creating, with our own hands, something in the chain that results in the capture of a fish. When so many people today are in jobs that do not allow them to be creative with their hands, the making and mending of fishing tackle can have a therapeutic effect.

Fly Fishing is Good for Us

When we are out fishing we breathe the clean country air, we get exercise, we extend our minds, and we certainly sleep better after a day at the waterside.

There is a great camaraderie among fly fishers that genuinely breaks all boundaries of colour, creed, class and race. It only needs two people to learn that they are both fly anglers for social barriers to be broken down and new friendships formed. There is so much to discuss, so many notes to be compared, so many experiences to relate, and so many theories to be propounded, that most anglers never seem to be at a loss for words.

It is a sport that can be enjoyed by the young, the middle aged, the elderly, and the disabled. So long as we can get out and wave a fly rod, there is no reason why we should not fish. Many participant sports close as age progresses and agility decreases, but not so with fly fishing. I have known some very frail and arthritic anglers who have been reduced to spending most of their time trailing their flies from the boat, as casting has become almost impossible, but if they can still enjoy themselves fishing in this way in their final years, then good luck to them. The provision of 'Wheelyboats' enables wheelchair-bound anglers to fish at ease and in safety. For an up-to-date list of UK fisheries that have Wheelyboats for hire, visit the website www.wheelyboats.org.

Wheelyboats for disabled anglers are appearing at more trout fisheries around the country.

Both men and women can participate in the sport, and if the ladies manage to 'outfish' the gentlemen as a result of their superior talents it is a spur to improve. More ladies are taking up fly fishing these days, which is a good thing.

Our sport is one that takes place over a longer timescale than most, and in the present day rat race, where it seems that everything has to be done at speed, it is good to be able to take our time and do things at a more leisurely pace. With most sports one cannot take a break without missing out on the action, but we are fortunate that we can stop for a breather and then carry on again whenever we wish.

Fly fishing is a sport that can be enjoyed at a moment's notice, and we are not reliant upon finding a partner or being a member of a team in order to go fishing. Although our destination may be an hour or so away, we can pack the car on an impulse and go. Unlike the coarse angler who needs a fresh supply of bait, fly fishers have all that is necessary in their fly boxes.

Fly fishing has standards of etiquette and sportsmanship that originate from a time when courteous behaviour was more valued than perhaps it is today. In a world that seems to be becoming increasingly undisciplined, insecure and even perilous, there is something reassuring about participating in a sport so deeply rooted in traditional values.

Lastly, but by no means least, the trout is a delicious fish to eat. It is a fish that can be cooked in so many different ways, and it is one that both tastes good, and one that medical science tells us is good for us (at least so far!). What better way can there be to end a day spent on the water than by savouring a freshly cooked trout that we have caught ourselves with a glass of chilled

Many advertisements and mail-order catalogues seem to show pretty young ladies fly fishing, and if that is an encouragement to both sexes to fish, what is wrong with that? (Photo courtesy of Hardy & Greys Ltd.)

champagne or sparkling white wine. And then, when we are suitably replete, retiring to bed to dream and relive the capture of that most magnificent of creatures, the trout.

Yes, on reflection, there is no doubt at all that fly fishing for trout really is the greatest sport known to mankind!

2   Tackle: Rods and Fly Lines

To complete any task successfully it is essential to possess the correct tools for the job, to have the necessary skills to be able to use them efficiently, to have an understanding of exactly what the task is and what we are trying to do and, finally, to possess the mental powers to enable us to overcome any unforeseen difficulties that will inevitably arise along the way.

Chapters 2, 3 and 5 deal with the items of tackle needed and how to make the best choices, so that they can serve us best in our endeavours to improve catch rates significantly.

Although it is assumed that the aspiring angler will possess sufficient tackle to have made a start in the sport, each component part will be looked at in turn, to try and ensure that we are using an efficient and comprehensive set of fish-catching tools. These will be examined in some considerable detail because, to get the maximum results from our efforts, it is necessary to make certain that every single link in the chain is capable of working at peak performance and that it is in peak condition.

After a time, experience tells us what tackle is essential and what suits us, and what is either superfluous or plain useless. Sadly, a great number of gimmicky innovations fall into this latter category. The author possesses numerous items bought on impulse that will never be used again.

Buy the Best

Buy good quality tackle every time; it is cheapest in the long run and it saves the problem of what to do with all the useless clutter we seem to accumulate. There is nothing worse than being let down by inadequate tackle, either because it fails at the crucial time, or because it is incapable of performing the tasks demanded of it. It is always the best conditioned and heaviest fish, and hence the ones that give the ultimate satisfaction in catching them if we are successful, that demand the maximum in performance. If your kit isn't 100 per cent efficient then change it or modify it, because otherwise the fish will inevitably exploit its weaknesses.

Reservoir Rods

Today the modern fly fisherman is very fortunate that the range of rods designed specifically for reservoir work is now extremely wide, and there are models that cater for every aspiration, and the depths of all pockets.

There is only one material used for the manufacture of fly rods that needs to be considered nowadays and that is carbon fibre (sometimes called graphite). It has become comparatively cheap, and it produces rods that are much lighter and much better than 30 years ago. A glance through the pages of the mail-order catalogues

With the possibility of encountering fish like this, quality tackle is essential. George Knight of Stanion with the biggest rainbow trout to come out of Eyebrook Reservoir to date. It weighed 20lb 13oz and was caught from the bank on a home-tied damsel nymph and is on display in the fishing lodge.

will give some idea of the vast choice now available.

For the sake of simplicity and uniformity, a lightweight 10ft fly rod with a tip to middle action, and rated at no. 7/8, will cover all needs, whether they are from the bank or the boat. The handle should be of the full wells type, as that is the one where the thumb can firmly grip the cork for maximum power and distance. Two stripping rings are better than one, and if the rod you fancy has two so much the better. Used in conjunction with a no. 8 rated line, you will have a kit that will send out a 20ft leader carrying a team of four lightweight flies with ease, or alternatively will punch out a heavily weighted goldhead or fry pattern into a head wind if needed, with both rigs landing in a straight line. What is more, at the end of the day you will not be totally exhausted. Fatigued from mental exhilaration and concentration maybe, but not physically exhausted! This outfit would suit

an average-build male angler, but a slightly built or elderly man, or a lady angler, may perhaps wish to go down a size in both rod and line.

To see how fly rods have become so much lighter over recent years, I put two similar rods (there was a variation in length of 2in) on to the scales to see the difference in weight between a modern lightweight carbon fibre rod and a split cane reservoir rod of 40 years ago. The results were startling.

With the sort of tools we were using 40 years ago, it is no wonder that we were all

Comparison in weight between split cane and carbon fibre fly rods

Rod	Weight (oz)
Davenport & Fordham T.C. Ivens Ravensthorpe 9ft 4in no. 6 split cane rod	6.35
Airflo Original Classic 9ft 6in no. 7/8 carbon fibre rod	3.46

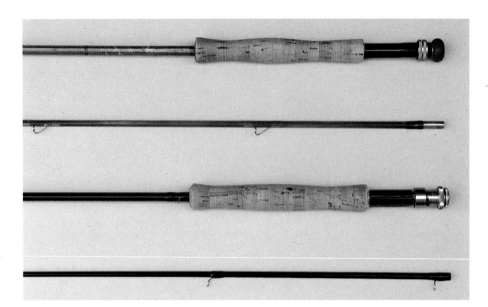

Two reservoir fly rods: traditional split cane (top) and carbon fibre (below).

totally worn out after a full day's fishing from the banks at Eyebrook Reservoir!

When buying a new rod, always try it out before purchase by casting with the line you intend to use. That is the only sure way to be certain that it is suitable. If buying by mail order, make sure that the company offer a no quibble return and refund policy if you are not 100 per cent satisfied.

These days there is no benefit in making one's own fly rod as the fully finished item is relatively cheap, whereas buying all the component parts – rod blank, rings, handle, reel seat and all the extras – is comparatively expensive. Also, you cannot be sure that you will be getting precisely what you expected until the rod is finished, and by then it will be too late.

Always carry your rods in a rod tube. Do not rely on a cloth bag and endeavouring to be careful because they inevitably do get knocks from time to time, especially in the boats. Mine is home-made from a holdall rod tube with caps on each end and a carrying handle whipped on to the middle; it takes two, two-piece fly rods in their cloth bags easily. It is quite battered and damaged

now and well overdue for replacement, but without it goodness knows what damage the rods might have suffered.

Fly Lines

After looking at fly rods the next logical item to discuss is the fly line, to see what is necessary if we are to have a range of tools to enable us to tackle every situation likely to be encountered.

For reservoir work there is only one profile of fly line that needs to be considered seriously – the weight forward taper. Stillwater fly fishing is all about endeavouring to catch a fish at some considerable distance from the angler, and therefore long-range casting to place the flies in its vicinity is essential.

We read a lot about the different designs and configurations of weight forward or torpedo tapers, but in essence they all boil down to the same thing. The weight needed to flex and load the rod is aerialized outside the tip ring, and the thin running line is pulled out by it as far as we need or we can manage when we shoot line. Long-distance casting is a necessity for the reservoir man and will be discussed in Chapter 4.

Whilst it is true that shooting heads offer the ultimate in casting distances, they do bring with them the problem of tangling, the difficulty in retrieving line in the hand, and setting the hook at great distances with stretchy shooting line can be problematic. It is therefore suggested that until the angler becomes more proficient they are best disregarded.

A floating line may be the only line that the beginner possesses at the outset, and a floater may be all that is necessary for much of the time. However, to become a versatile performer the possession of a range of different density fly lines is essential, in order that the different layers of water that the trout may be using may be exploited at the appropriate time. We next look at fly lines in general.

The Advantages of Modern Plastic Fly Lines

In the old days of silk fly lines, anglers had, in effect, only one type of fly line to use – the floater. Although by its very nature it was prone to sinking as its specific gravity was denser than water, it was possible to make it float as a result of greasing it and the

A selection of British and American floating and sinking fly lines together with two disc drag cartridge reservoir fly reels by BFR.

effect of surface tension. After a period of time, however, it then became waterlogged and started to sink; it had to be re-dressed to make it float again. As a consequence, anglers were usually loathe to let them sink in the first place.

Today we are blessed with the benefits of modern technology, which has given fly line manufacturers the ability to produce, and reproduce accurately, lines with a wide variety of densities. The floating ones will float continuously, without the need for any dressing, as a consequence of them being lighter than water, and the sinking ones will sink consistently as a result of them being heavier. In comparison with silk lines, they are virtually maintenance free, although a careful cleaning and dressing each outing will make them perform better and last longer. The varying densities of sinkers that are produced nowadays means that the speed of sinking can be controlled precisely, so that a line can be chosen to match the requirements that tactics dictate on the day.

This means that we are now spoilt for choice, with a bewildering array of densities available, and it is necessary to try and rationalize the alternatives so that we possess sufficient types for our needs, but not so many as to confuse matters unnecessarily. The advent of braided and polymer leaders

The difficulty of seeing the end of a fly line 25yd away. Inset: tip of fly line enlarged.

has given anglers the facility to fine-tune the sinking rates, and hence the depths that the flies fish, and so vast numbers of lines for the majority of anglers are an unnecessary complication (and expense).

Fly Line Colour

When thinking about the colour of fly lines, perhaps the primary feature to consider is that it should be as inconspicuous as possible and thus give the trout no cause for alarm. Colours such as olive, green and other drab colours, which either blend into the surroundings or else will be camouflaged to some extent by them, are a wise choice for floaters and intermediates; with the darker greens and browns being appropriate for the same reasons for sinkers.

Due to the long distances that reservoir anglers cast, and also the fact that the tip portions of all floaters tend to sink anyway, the very bright and fluorescent colours cannot be seen properly by an angler who is probably 25yd away and so they give little benefit. To the fish who will be swimming in the vicinity of them, however, such unnatural colours, ones that they would never encounter in the normal state of things, must make them suspicious, curious, or even positively alarmed.

After giving the matter a great deal of thought I shall be disregarding all the manufacturers' claims about line visibility, and in future will be looking for drab, natural colours when buying any new fly lines and fully anticipate catches to increase as a result.

Dispelling the Confusion

Although the manufacturers would want us to believe that we cannot do without their latest line offering, this is certainly not the case and we need not be swayed by such claims. That is not to say that we do not

need to keep up with new technology, but we do need to avoid the temptation of buying every new season's improvement. If a line works well and catches sufficient fish, why change it for the sake of it before it has worn out – especially at £40 or £50 a time?

To simplify matters, the number of lines will be narrowed down to a handful, which will cover the needs of most reservoir fly fishermen. Although every angler's requirements will differ to some degree, the lines discussed will cover 95 per cent of most fishing needs, and the remaining 5 per cent can be catered for by a sensible compromise.

Match anglers, in their never-ending quest to achieve even a slight advantage over other competitors, would no doubt consider the range discussed here to be far too limited and decide to carry more.

Floating Lines

A floater must be the most important line by far, and for the vast bulk of fishing time it will be the most appropriate choice. The author does suggest that a quality line for this application should be purchased if at all possible, and although the best lines are not cheap you generally do get what you pay for. If economies have to be made, it should be in the area of sinking lines, where optimum performance is not always quite so important.

Providing the wind (or lack of it) does not complicate matters, for all surface and sub-surface fishing a floating line must be first choice for presentation, bite detection, ease of lift off, casting, and for the sheer pleasure of use. It is probable that there are some anglers around who fish throughout the entire season with virtually nothing else.

Intermediate Lines

Next we will discuss a slow intermediate or neutral density line. (The term 'neutral

Match fisherman and England International Graham Herbert with a magnificent 6lb 4oz rainbow taken from Heathcote Lake in Warwickshire on a Daddy Long Legs.

density' is somewhat misleading. Water has a density of exactly 1.0, a modern floating line has a density of less than 1.0, an intermediate line has a density of slightly more than 1.0, and a sinker has a density greater than 1.0.) This line can prove very useful when there is a strong surface wind or cross current, when a floater would tend to skate across the surface and drag the flies with it in a most unnatural manner. An intermediate line, sunk just below the surface in these conditions, will be much more stable and will virtually eliminate the problem. When the flies need to be fished just that little bit deeper they are again the ideal choice.

As intermediate lines sink under the water rather than lay on the surface, in flat calm conditions, when the trout can see fly lines and everything else very clearly, they do not seem to alarm the fish to such a great extent as floaters. These lines are, in fact, sinkers, albeit with very slow sink rates, and given enough time they will eventually reach the bottom. At the present time there is no line that will truly stay poised just below the surface but without breaking the surface film, and no doubt line manufacturers are working hard on this one.

A fast intermediate line is the next choice for presenting the flies somewhat deeper below the surface or in mid water, when, for example, ascending buzzer pupae or other nymphs are being taken on their way to the surface to hatch, and in such circumstances it can be an extremely useful line. On those occasions when there is a need for a faster retrieve rate, which brings with it the problem of line wake when using a floating line, they often prove to be an ideal solution.

Sinking Lines

The next two lines, which will be considered together, are a medium sinker and a fast sinker. They will generally be of greater use to the boat angler than to his counterpart on the bank, unless he is fishing from the dam wall or into deep water. Their main use will be to fish a lure quickly to prevent the flies from surfacing. Other applications are for nymph fishing in mid water and for fishing near the bottom either in early or late season during cold weather, or at the other extreme in hot summer weather when the fish have retired to deeper water.

Counting down the sink rate of the line until the productive taking level is found is a valuable technique, and when the time taken for intermediate lines to descend to the desired level is overlong, medium and fast sinkers will save valuable fishing time. When fishing from a drifting boat, using a sinking line helps to overcome the problem of overrunning the flies before they have sunk to the desired working depth, something that can occur when fishing with a floating line.

Ultra Fast Sinkers

The final essential line, which is a unique one for specialized applications, is the ultra fast sinker. It is used for booby fishing either from the bank or a boat, for getting the flies down very deep, very quickly from a drifting boat, for deep lure fishing, or for 'back-drifting' a booby trailed behind the boat. There is no other line available that will perform any of these functions satisfactorily.

Very high density lines can be more difficult to cast, requiring a controlled action and more precise timing, but on those occasions that demand their use nothing else will do.

The Profile of Sinking Fly Lines

Depending on their density, different sinking rate fly lines will take on a different profile in the water as they sink, and how they behave as they are pulled through the water will be distinctly different as well. A line that sinks at 2in per second after a countdown of 40sec will *not* have the same profile in the water as one that sinks at 4in per second after a 20sec countdown. They may both be fishing at the same depth, but the path that the line adopts in the water will not be the same.

This point was reinforced only recently whilst boat fishing in mid October. After fishing without result for a couple of hours with a fast sinker, the line was exchanged for an intermediate one. The first time it was cast out, after allowing plenty of time for the line to sink whilst pouring out a cup of coffee, the rod was picked up and after three or four slow draws a fish was 'on' straightaway. A countdown of 60sec was repeated, and during a period of just over an hour three more fish were in the bag. Although both lines were being fished at the same depth, in some way the presentation was evidently different to such an extent that one way was acceptable to the trout whilst the other was not.

Keeping in Contact with the Fish

I do not take too much notice of the advertising claims about density-compensated sinking fly lines and the profile that they take in the water. When a fish 'pulls' or the angler tightens up in response to a take, the line is drawn through the water in the way that it would if it were being pulled through a length of tubing, rather than actually straightening any curve in the line. Due to the comparatively large diameters of fly lines it is much harder to straighten out any curve whereas simply sliding it through the water is relatively resistance free. Try the simple test of pulling a loop of 5yd of sunk line quickly through the water and you will get some idea of the water resistance. What *is* important is that contact is maintained with the flies at all times and that slack line is avoided. Keeping in touch with the terminal tackle will put many more fish in the bag.

A Versatile Set of Tools

The six lines listed should form the basis of a very versatile set of fishing tools that will cope with virtually every reservoir fishing situation ashore or afloat, without breaking the bank. At a later stage, purchasing an extra line to fit a specific situation that may be regularly encountered might be considered necessary, for example a sink tip or a shooting head, but these six lines will provide a good, solid foundation upon which to build.

It may be considered that the next line to be bought might well be another floater, giving the angler the versatility of being able to have two rods with floating lines set up at the same time, for example one with a team of nymphs and the other with dries or emergers.

It is desirable to possess at least two reels of identical design with enough interchangeable

Typical range of sinking speeds of various fly line densities

Fly line type	Sinking speed in inches per second
Floating	0
Slow intermediate/neutral	0.6–1.2
Fast intermediate	1.25–1.75
Medium sinking	2.5–3.0
Fast sinking	3.0–4.0
Ultra fast sinking	6.0–8.0

matching spools to carry all the lines, as well as two rods, as this enables quick change-overs to be made simply by putting down one rod and picking up another. This saves all the bother of threading lines and changing leaders and flies whenever a change of tactics is being tried, and it takes only a few seconds rather than minutes.

Changing Lines when Fishing

The simplest way of threading a different line up a rod that has already been set up with a leader and flies is to wind the line in until the bob fly is almost at the tip ring, and then to thread the new line up the rings alongside the old one, and before the new reel has been attached to the rod. It is essential to ensure that in the haste of doing this no rings have been accidentally overlooked! When the existing braided or polymer leader is reached, the nylon leader is cut from the old line and immediately tied on to the braided or polymer leader of the new one. The old fly line can then be wound back on to its reel and removed from the rod and the new reel fixed in its place.

It sounds a more complicated operation to perform than it actually is, and for maximum efficiency the procedure should be practised at home a few times to get it right

Barrie Thompson of Whitwell with an 8lb 3oz rainbow from Eyebrook Reservoir, which took a Black Buzzer fished on a floating line.

before trying it out on the bank or in the boat. The method does eliminate to some extent the problem of the leader blowing around and getting tangled.

Cleaning Fly Lines Regularly

If you want to ensure that your fly lines last more than a couple of seasons, why not make a resolution to clean, dress and straighten them after every outing. It only takes a few minutes to do this once the routine becomes second nature, and the benefits are enormous.

To start with you need to make a line twist remover, which consists of a ball-bearing swivel with a snap link attached to one eye. To the other eye, tie a 24in loop of backing with a split ring on it.

When you need to use it, loop the cord round a post and put the swivel through the split ring to secure it and you are ready. (I use the street lamp outside and do get funny looks from passers-by, but we anglers are strange folk anyway!)

Remove the braided or polymer leader from the fly line and attach the braided loop at the end of the fly line to the snap

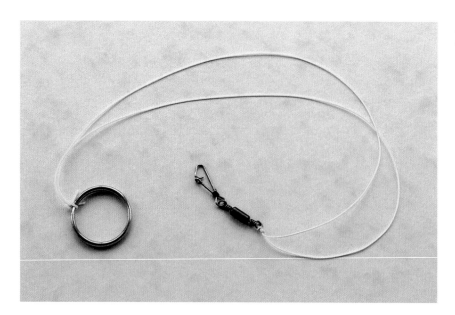

Ball-bearing fly line twist remover.

link and then unwind the full length of fly line. When the line is fully unwound, give it a good stretch of a couple of feet or so and this will remove any line twist and also straighten the line (the cause and cure for line twist is dealt with in Chapter 4). The ball-bearing swivel is much more efficient than a cheap one for removing line twist. Stretching the line whilst it is twisted in any way will seriously damage it, and it will never be straight again, so it is as well to take this simple precaution.

Place the reel on any convenient support so that all the line is off the ground (you may have to tighten the drag to do this) and then run a few drops of your chosen line cleaner, on a small felt pad, up and down the line a couple of times, starting initially at the backing end. Clean off any surplus dressing by lightly running a clean felt pad

down the line just once. When this has been done, slacken off the drag on the reel to its original setting and wind the line gently back on to the reel, using only the tension of picking it up off the ground, on to preferably a large arbor reel or alternatively a standard reel with just enough backing to almost fill it with the line loosely wound, and then you are ready for next time.

Not only will you find that the line will now literally zip through the rod rings like a brand new one, giving significantly greater casting distances, but it will also lie dead straight on the water, giving far better bite detection and contact with the fish, and an instant lifting into any trout that takes.

If you look after your lines in this way, you will fish more efficiently, your lines will last longer, and in turn this will save you money.

3   Tackle: Reels and Accessories

After looking at two of the three most important items of fly fishing tackle in the previous chapter (the other one is the fly hook, which will be discussed in Chapter 14), the rest of what is needed will now be considered.

The Reservoir Fly Reel

The main properties of a good reservoir fly reel are quite straightforward: it should be sturdy, take the required line size plus 75–100yd of backing, have a large diameter, preferably by possessing a large arbor, have an exposed rim that can be used as a brake, and it should have interchangeable spools that can be exchanged speedily for all the fly lines that it is intended to use.

It is important to take time initially over the decision of which reel to use and then to stick to it. Employing reels with a cartridge type of spool system is quick, efficient and replacement spools are exceedingly good value.

The incorporation of a disc drag is something that, although others may disagree, the author considers to be an unnecessary expense. He prefers to control a running fish, which is taking line from the spool (sadly not a very frequent occurrence), by braking the reel using finger pressure on the rim. It is much safer and makes you feel like you are actually playing the fish rather than sitting back and letting the reel do the

job. In normal circumstances, a hooked trout should be played by hand lining rather than by winding the reel – even with a large arbor it is impossible to wind fast enough to keep in touch with a fish swimming towards you.

Reels can cost anything from a few pounds up to many hundreds, and it is up to the angler to use his budget wisely according to the depth of his pocket. Having said that, possessing a well-engineered bar stock reel may not be essential, but having one can give immense pleasure in both ownership and use.

Using different designs of reels not only costs more money in the long run, but it can also waste valuable fishing time when the trout are moving. Having just one reel type, one with which the angler is thoroughly familiar, enables it to be used without the worry of having to think about which type is in use at the time. It is important to be thoroughly at ease with all one's fishing tackle and the reel is no different. When a big fish is 'on' is not the time to be wondering where the drag knob is!

The spools should be filled with sufficient backing so that, with the fly line fitted and loosely wound on, the reel is comfortably full. This will reduce memory coils and also give added security if a fish should take line.

Fly reels are precision-engineered pieces of equipment that can be damaged if not looked after properly. They deserve to be protected from injury, so always keep them in a padded reel pouch when not in use. At the end of the season, wash and dry them carefully and lubricate them in accordance with the maker's instructions before putting them away. If this is done they should last for many years.

Landing Nets

The specification for the ideal net is basically simple. It should be as *big* as possible, have a deep knotless mesh, a long handle, and possess a spike on the end for sticking into the ground or reservoir when bank fishing.

To elaborate a little, the diameter of the ring should be at least 24in. That size makes netting a relatively simple procedure, with no more trying to guide a big fish where it doesn't want to go. Trout don't seem to want to fold up to fit puny nets; they want to evade them at any opportunity they can get.

One feature that most boat nets do not seem to possess, and which would be a vast improvement, is that they should float. Not particularly space-age technology one would think, but it would save a

A selection of reservoir landing nets. The largest shown has a net ring diameter of 26in.

lot of frustration and expense should the inevitable come to pass. There is simply no way that a trout can be brought into a boat without a net.

Fly Boxes

Ethafoam-lined fly boxes will take the flies without damaging the hooks, they are cheap, and are recommended. If they should happen to get wet, put them in the airing cupboard to dry out *immediately* upon returning home. This will prevent the hooks from rusting.

I carry three separate fly boxes: one for nymphs and marabou flies, one for dry flies, and one for goldheads, lures, fry patterns, muddlers and boobies. Spending time going through the fly boxes from time to time, clearing the hook eyes of dirt and monofil, checking for damage to the dressings, and discarding any flies where the hook is rusted or damaged in any way, is a discipline that is well worth practising and may save heartache later on. An end-of-season sort out of the contents is a wise plan, as those flies that do not produce fish seem to proliferate because they never get used up, whereas successful flies seem to disappear as a result of getting damaged, being lost, or by being given away. This will ensure that the productive flies and not the duffers predominate.

To keep flies in peak condition it is a wise precaution to keep fly boxes closed whilst fishing, as exposure to sunlight quickly causes natural and dyed materials to fade and fluorescent ones to lose their brilliance. A supply of bead head pins liberally distributed throughout the fly boxes to clear blocked hook eyes and for unravelling knots is a useful provision. It seems that you cannot have too many!

Accessories

There are so many accessories to part the angler from his hard-earned money that it is wise to make sure that we do not burden ourselves with unnecessary cost and weight. Those things that are essential are:

- Polarized spectacles: for eye protection and for seeing into the water.
- Leader wallet containing spare leaders and spare monofil. Leaders and leader materials will be looked at in depth in Chapter 5.
- A pair of artery forceps for removing deeply hooked flies.
- Priest.
- Marrow spoon (*see* Chapter 9).
- A shallow dish for examining the results of autopsies.
- Hook sharpener.
- Leader straightener for restoring kinked line.
- Snips or scissors on a zinger for trimming leader material.
- Amadou or some other implement for drying waterlogged flies.
- Containers of leader sinkant, fly floatant, line grease, and one of the crystal preparations for drying out soggy flies.
- Bass bag: for that trout!
- Small towel for drying hands.
- Notebook and pencil.
- Rod licence and ticket money.
- Mobile phone (in order that other anglers are not disturbed it is suggested that it is only used for emergencies).
- 'Reserve' tin containing torch, whipping thread, insulating tape, penknife, tube of superglue, small screwdriver, sun lotion, minor first-aid kit and other infrequently used odds and ends.

The following items are not essential, but the angler might wish to take some of them along with him:

- Magnifying glass and pocket guide to insect identification if you wish to take your entomology a little further.
- Camera.
- De-barbing pliers if catch and release is practised.
- Thermometer.
- Binoculars.
- Set of dry clothes in case of a soaking.

Tackle Bags

After putting up with what are claimed to be 100 per cent waterproof tackle bags, with their so-called waterproof linings, taped seams and so on, but which in reality let water in through the base, the flaps, the zips and everywhere else, I have now decided to abandon them in favour of the humble moulded plastic Shakespeare blue coarse fisher's tackle box for boat fishing.

For the first time ever I now have something that is rigid, takes all my gear comfortably and in some semblance of order, and does not let water in through the base. Virtually no water penetrates through the lid, even when it has been standing in the boat for several hours in torrential rain. You can also sit on it. Thankfully, long gone are the days when I used to have to take all my kit out and dry it out after a day in the rain. It may not be as trendy as the purpose-built fly fishing bags with their 'designer' tags, but

Moulded plastic seat box for boat fishing.

it stores my spare reels and spools, waterproofs, drogues, spare clothing, camera, fishfinder, flask and lunch box, as well as various minor odds and ends, with ease. It was also far cheaper than any of my leaky fabric bags.

When choosing a tackle box, it is important to get one that is large enough to take all you need. With that, however, comes the temptation to carry more and more tackle simply because it will fit in. This only adds to the weight to be carried around. If, like me, you like travelling as light as possible, it is a good idea to go through your tackle from time to time and, if any item has not been used for a while, decide whether it is really necessary to carry it.

When bank fishing, I still take the boat box along in the car boot and simply transfer what is needed into a large plastic handyman's tool box, one fitted with both a carrying handle and a shoulder strap, which is carried down to the water. Everything is kept dry, and it can be used as a seat at a pinch.

Clothing

Sensible clothing for fly fishing should be warm, comfortable and suitable for the anticipated weather. In order that the fish are not alarmed it should be in green, olive, brown or some other drab colour. The use of polarized glasses, as a safety precaution against a wayward fly striking the eye, should be mandatory for everyone who values their eyesight.

Wearing a long peaked hat cuts out the glare from overhead and so makes studying the water and spotting fish much easier. In wet weather, wearing a baseball cap with a long peak underneath a waterproof hat will keep the head dry and will stop the problem of rain forming droplets on the glasses. With British weather being as unpredictable as it is, carrying a waterproof jacket with a hood and a pair of waterproof overtrousers at all times is a must.

For fishing in cold, early and late season weather, a set of thermal underwear comprising a long-sleeved top and a pair of full-length trousers, made from one of the new materials that wicks moisture away from the skin, keeping the body warm, dry and comfortable, is essential. It contributes not only to the enjoyment of unseasonal days, but also to increased fishing efficiency. The modern trend of utilizing several layers of clothing is now established as the most practical way of accommodating the variations in weather conditions, and the angler only has to add or remove a layer as comfort demands and the weather dictates.

Waterproof footwear is necessary whether fishing from the bank or from a boat. When boat fishing, water enters the boat every time a fish is landed, the anchor is raised, the drogue is pulled in, or simply when it rains, and keeping the feet dry is essential for comfort. A baling pump (if one is fitted) is a boon and in addition some implement for baling out water (and other personal needs) will be required for keeping the boat dry. On the bank we will be confronted by mud, puddles and wet grass, even if we are not wading, and waterproof footwear to keep the feet dry and warm will be necessary.

Food and Drink

I like to fish rather than waste a lot of time eating and drinking, so a flask of hot coffee, supplemented by a bottle of spring water in hot weather, usually suffices for liquid refreshment. A few freshly made sandwiches to keep me going during the day, until arriving home for a proper meal in the evening, is all I seem to need. Although some folk enjoy making a leisurely picnic of their fishing days, I generally find that I am far too busy with my fishing to pay much

Caught napping after one of my wife's fishing picnics! Fishing should always be fun, so why not relax after lunch?

thought to the inner man. Keeping hungry seems to galvanize that hunter–gather instinct in me.

However, on occasion, when the weather is good, my wife will arrive at lunch time with one of her renowned picnics: smoked salmon parcels, Melton Mowbray pork pie, cold meats, buttered fresh split white rolls, crisps, scones and a 'Death by Chocolate' dessert, all with a half bottle of 'Blanc de Noir' to round it off. After that the afternoon's fishing generally seems to disappear into a bit of a blur!

Waders and Bank Gear

On many reservoirs, thigh waders are the only kind that are allowed. As most of the reservoirs have mud bottoms, or occasionally muddy gravel, generally speaking cleated soles will be the best choice for a good grip, but waters do vary.

Rubber, PVC, neoprene, nylon and many different breathable materials are all used, and it is often the depth of one's pocket that is the deciding factor. The equation that has to be considered is whether to spend a lot of money on an expensive pair of waders in the hope that they will last, or alternatively to purchase a cheaper pair and subsequently replace them more regularly? On balance, I think I prefer the latter.

The waders should be hung upside down in a cool, dark place to dry out after every single use. A pair of simple wader hangers is still the best device to make sure that cracking, which happens as a result of them being stored folded, is eliminated. Waders never seem to last as long as we would like, but we should do all we can to extend their useful life for as long as possible. If they should get punctured, one of the wader repair kits will prolong their life for a while, but once they start to wear out it is time for replacement. They should never be left in the car boot in between fishing trips as the resulting creasing and high temperatures are the surest way to ruin them.

Line Tray

Although they are not seen often these days, a line tray or stripping basket is a must for the reservoir bank angler, for they can add 3 or 4yd to an average cast. They also eliminate the ever present hazard of line dropped on the ground catching on twigs, stubble or other debris, which can result in a spoiled cast as well as frustration. The use of a line tray also avoids the possibility of treading on an expensive line and either damaging it or possibly cutting it in half.

As I always use a line tray when wading, I have not experienced the tragedy of a fish that is being brought close in to be netted suddenly diving through the loose coils of line and the dire consequences that brings.

Boat Gear

Boat fishing brings with it the necessity for more specialized gear than the bank man needs, and which, unfortunately, is heavy and has to be carried down to the boat.

Some kind of comfortable fishing seat is essential. If you suffer with a bad back like me, a swivel seat with webbing that is strapped to the boat board is a boon. Some boat seats are very low, leading to the knees being drawn up, with resultant back pains at the end of the day. The author

has fabricated a wooden block 3¾in thick, which goes between the bottom plate of the swivel seat and the boat board, raising the whole thing to a more comfortable fishing height. Details of its construction are given in Appendix II.

Unfortunately, not all boats have seats that can accommodate a webbing type of arrangement. Some have integrally moulded seats with no gap through which the webbing can be threaded, and in such circumstances the seat needs to be clamped to a thwart board.

Wooden boat seat riser block. Dimensions are 21in × 7in × 3¾in.

Webbing-to-clamp seat device. It raises the fishing height by 2½in.

For this kind of boat, the author has produced a device that allows the webbing to be attached to it, with the clamp-type fitting attached below, which in turn grips the seat of the boat. Details of its construction are also given in Appendix II. Clamp devices are not as secure as webbing.

Drogues for slowing down the drift are now manufactured in decent sizes and easily available. Remember to attach it to the boat *before* throwing it over the side unless you want to replace it regularly!

Having an anchor of your own attached to 10ft of chain, with a detachable weight that can be clipped on or removed as necessary, tied to 100ft of floating polypropylene rope on its own winder, and kept in a bag in the boot of the car is a wise precaution. If the one provided by the fishery proves to be unsuitable it can be fetched and brought into use. If the wind is such that the anchor will not hold without dragging, it is perhaps wise to consider whether one should be boat fishing at all, at least in the present location.

A life jacket of some sort is *essential* when going afloat and *it should be worn at all times*. By far the most useful life jacket in many circumstances is the fly vest which incorporates an automatic inflation device and so makes a separate life jacket unnecessary. There are designs that incorporate numerous pockets to carry the angler's fly boxes, leader materials, priest, and other odds and ends, and they do encourage the discipline of ensuring that the angler wears it at all times. Getting into the habit of putting tackle away into the same pocket every time will ensure that it can be located easily when required. It should go without saying, but needs repeating judging by the number of times one sees folk fishing with them undone, that life jackets *must* be correctly clipped and/or zipped up to function properly in the event of an emergency. I wear mine at all times, whether bank fishing or boat fishing, without exception.

Electric outboard motors and their use are discussed in Chapter 12.

Electronic Fishfinders

There is probably no piece of equipment employed by fly fishermen that is as controversial as the electronic fishfinder. To some they are a useful fishing aid, and to others they give a distinctly unfair advantage. Usually their detractors base their accusations on an incomplete knowledge of exactly what they can and what they cannot do. In simple terms, they will give the angler extra information that he can use to base his fishing tactics on:

- The depth of the water.
- The underwater contours.
- Any bottom features, structure or weed beds.
- Whether the bottom is hard (rocky) or soft (muddy or weedy).
- Whether there are fish in the vicinity and if so approximately what size they are and at what depth they are. They will *not* tell him whether they are trout or coarse fish, in which direction they are travelling or whether they are feeding or not!

They most definitely do not enable one to spot a fish, cast to it, and subsequently catch it without giving the matter any thought. In reality there is much information that they do not give. They can also be deceptive, for example when fish are cruising high in the water they will go around the boat and not under it to register on the transducer, which as a consequence will record nothing. To the unthinking angler using one, and not observing what is going on around

An American-made Eagle fishfinder.

him, an area which is seemingly devoid of fish could in reality be stuffed with them.

In summary, used judiciously, especially on a water that the angler does not know well, they can be very useful and can help him build up a picture of the water much more quickly. On the other hand, used without thought they can be unhelpful and even positively misleading. In spite of their usefulness, the fact does remain that to date the author's fastest limit, eight fish in under 2hr fishing, was taken on a day when he was not using one. Make of that what you may.

Tackle Checklist

With all the kit that is needed, it is a sound plan to have a tackle checklist hanging up in the garage, which is referred to as the gear is loaded into the car. This will ensure that nothing is left behind. There can be nothing more disheartening than to arrive at the waterside only to discover that one's waders are still at home! I have not left a vital item of kit at home to date, but I can

remember in my coarse fishing days arriving at the water without any bait.

Whilst on the subject of tackle storage, it is a wise precaution to bring fly boxes and fly lines inside the house over the winter months, rather than leave them in cold and damp garages or sheds where hooks may possibly become rusty and fly lines lose their plasticity and crack.

Conclusions

Fishing should always be fun, and that is one of the primary objectives of all that we do. Having a set of tackle comprehensive enough to cope with most situations, but without being unnecessarily over-complicated and weighing us down more than necessary, does enable that aim to be fulfilled.

Good quality tackle is a pleasure to own and to use, and it can make the often difficult and trying task of attempting to deceive a wily and uncooperative trout a pleasure as well. Look after it and it will rarely let you down.

4 Casting and the Necessity for Distance

In reality, accomplished casting is a fundamental component of any branch of fly fishing, and when it comes specifically to reservoir fly fishing, where the distance that the trout may be from the angler can be considerable, it is even more important! If the fish are at a great distance from the angler and he is unable to reach them, then he is simply wasting his time. In no other branch of angling is the method of propelling the lure or bait achieved by utilizing the weight of the line, as opposed to the weight of the terminal tackle, and in consequence it is very different to any other.

The procedure of fly casting demands its own techniques, and as the reader will have found out if he has already made a start, it does not come as second nature. It is a method of propulsion that is foreign to us, and it has to be learnt and mastered. There are no easy shortcuts – apart from being correctly taught in the first place.

Distance Casting Demands Balanced Tackle

Possessing a rod and line that are perfectly matched for each other is *essential* for long-distance casting. Although the introduction of the American Fishing Tackle Manufacturers' Association (AFTM) system has made things much clearer, the claimed ratings of rods and lines are not always as accurate as one would hope and expect, which is why trying out tackle is imperative. (I am seriously beginning to question the established principle of taking into account only the weight of the fly line outside the rod tip as the basis for matching lines to rods. The weight that actually flexes the rod should surely include the (weight of) line between the rod tip down to where it is held at the rod handle. Rod rings are designed so that they offer as little friction as possible and so, in effect, we should consider the line to be a continuous length from hand to fly line tip. This observation may account for the reason why when using shooting heads it is usually necessary to go up a line size or two to load the rod properly.) If you are not sure that the rod and line that you propose to purchase are perfectly matched, ask an experienced angler to try them out for you and give his opinion before buying.

As an example of what can go wrong, I can remember in my early days struggling with a no. 6 rated split cane rod and a no. 6 shooting head, which in my ignorance I assumed would complement one another, but which did not cast at all. The rod never flexed nor produced any power. Only when I took advice from a professional tutor, who diagnosed the problem in an instant, did things improve. After he had tried the rod he suggested that I use a WF9F, which was the line rating necessary to make the rod work! Once this had been done, things improved dramatically and the rod cast a great line. Forty years on those sorts of mistakes are much rarer, but the experience is a salutary reminder.

As another example, a fly line purchased only recently did not load the rod properly. The belly was subsequently weighed on accurate digital scales and compared to another line that did load the rod correctly, and the reason became clear. The line was, in reality, more than one full size lighter than its claimed rating. It should not happen, but it sometimes does.

Two Important Casts

There are many different techniques of casting for fly anglers in general, but as reservoir fishermen are usually fishing either from clear banks with little in the way of obstructions, or from boats where there are none at all, most techniques are not relevant. They can safely be left to the river angler and the salmon fisher who may well need them in more trying conditions where bankside obstructions and the current can cause their own difficulties. If the angler wishes to learn more casts for his own pleasure and satisfaction that is to be encouraged, but they are not essential. The two casts that *are* essential for the reservoir angler are the overhead cast and the roll cast.

The Overhead Cast

This is the basic long-distance cast for delivering the flies, and it should be practised until it is as smooth, as effortless and as perfect as possible. Being able to perform an overhead cast properly is the basic necessity for any reservoir fly fisherman, no matter how long they have been in the game. More aspiring fly anglers probably give up because of a deficiency in this one department than all the others combined.

It is *essential* to be able to put out a decent line properly. This cannot be stressed too much. Practising can be difficult and frustrating, and you will get some funny comments from passers-by when you practise in the park ('Caught any yet, mister?'), but there is simply no substitute for getting it right. We may live in an age where everyone wants everything instantly, but the fact remains that casting skills only come with continual practice.

Let it be said at the outset that I do not subscribe to the fallacy that it is not essential to be able to cast a long line. It may sound encouraging to the novice who is unable to put out a long line to say the opposite, but it is simply untrue. To the contrary, any novice who *is* able to cast a respectable line must be at a distinct advantage over one who is restricted to short-line work. Most fish will be caught at a fair distance from the angler; that is an undisputable fact. We all catch fish at short range from time to time, especially from the boats, but such fish are the exception rather than the rule.

I am not suggesting that we need to be able to cast to the horizon to have any chance of success, but an absolute minimum of 20–25yd should be the aim of the bank fisherman, although somewhat less for the boat angler may suffice. With a little practice, this sort of distance should not be beyond the capability of most people. If you take a rod length of say 3yd, add another 12yd of aerialized line, 5yd for the line shot through the rod rings, and a further 5yd for the terminal tackle, the point fly will be 25yd away from the angler. That is not outside the capability of most with a successful cast in reasonable fishing conditions. With time and practice this distance should steadily improve.

Being able to put a long line out where other anglers cannot reach will put you in the position where the fish will be able to see your flies but no one else's – with obvious advantages.

Left-Hand Line Acceleration and the Double Haul

Applying left-hand acceleration to the fly line during the forward and the back casts will increase distance for very little effort. The pulls should be performed smoothly and without any jerky movements, which will only cause the line to snake. If the hauls are executed correctly, the fly line will flow in a straight line, which will result in the double benefits of greater casting distances and a reduction in the number of leader tangles. Tangles in the leader must surely be one of the greatest sources of frustration for newcomers – the author has undoubtedly spent more than his fair share of time sitting on the bank trying to undo the kind of bird's nests that would make untying the Gordian Knot seem like child's play!

If slack line is allowed to develop during the periods when power should be applied, it will only dissipate energy, which in turn reduces distance. It will also cause the line to snatch when all does finally become taut once again – very likely causing either wind knots or leader tangles. Slack line is the bane of the fly fisher at any time and so keeping the rod tip close to the surface when retrieving line – or even an inch or so below it in windy conditions – will enable any slight touch, nudge, pluck or enquiry by the fish to be registered by the hand. The angler who always holds his rod 2 or 3ft above the surface during the retrieve will miss a lot of tactile indications.

Learning the 'double haul' technique, used in conjunction with the overhead cast, should be attempted as soon as the angler is conversant with basic casting. It will not be needed all the time, but it will enable longer casts to be made in good conditions when they are required, or reasonable ones to be attained at those times when the air is still and dead and casting becomes harder work, or else when fishing into a head wind. The double haul is not difficult to learn, and can be mastered by anyone who can perform a basic overhead cast. It must surely be a natural progression for anyone who wants better fishing returns.

The Roll Cast

The second essential cast is the roll cast, and this is useful for getting the line on to the surface in front of the angler before the casting cycle begins. It can either be with the forward punch laying the line out on the water to be immediately picked off as the back cast is begun, or alternatively without the line touching the surface at all, but brought back smartly into the back cast before the line has had time to land. This latter method saves time and eliminates disturbance of the water immediately in front of the angler.

In comparison to the overhead cast, the roll cast is relatively easy to learn and can be mastered in a short time. Nevertheless, in spite of its simplicity it is an extremely useful cast to have at one's disposal.

When a trout is attempting to engulf the fly as the lift off is being started, and we are unable to draw in any more line because the rod is held high and the arm is fully extended behind, a quickly executed roll cast may hook the fish. If it does not, then a continuation of the roll cast will drop the fly straight down on its nose once again and at least give another chance.

Other casts can be added to the repertoire if the angler wishes, but for most reservoir scenarios the two casts discussed will suffice in most circumstances.

(a) Double hauling the line.

(b) Shooting line.

(c) Ready to start the retrieve. Keeping the rod tip close to the surface eliminates slack line.

Long distance casting. The ability to put out a long line is essential for any reservoir angler.

The wrist 'broken' on the back cast (left) and a wrist support in use (right).

Common Casting Faults

All of us make mistakes from time to time when casting. But the same ones probably dog us all.

Letting the rod drift back too far on the back cast is probably one of the most common faults that will develop, in the mistaken notion that it will result in more power, and therefore greater distance. This, however, causes wider loops and allows the line to drop behind the angler. It then has to be lifted again on the forward cast, using up valuable energy, which in turn reduces distance. One of the ways this can happen unintentionally is by 'breaking' the wrist on the back cast, instead of keeping it at an angle of no more than 30 degrees to the rod handle. If this is a problem, there are numerous wrist supports available into which the butt of the rod is tucked and which eliminate this fault at a stroke. It is surprising how much of an improvement this simple device can make. The photo-

graphs above show the cause and the cure for wrist 'break'.

Another common fault is letting out too much line when false casting, which only overloads the rod, restricts line shoot, can introduce line twist, and as a result cuts distance rather than increasing it.

Line twist, which is a fault normally associated with weight forward lines, leads to annoying tangles in the running line between the reel and the first stripper ring, and it is a casting fault rather than a defect in the fly line. It is caused when the weight forward section of the fly line is extended beyond the tip of the rod during the casting stroke, and then subsequently moving the rod tip in a circle rather than backwards and forwards when false casting. As a result the heavier weight forward section is rotating in a circle, putting a twist in the thinner and more flexible running line with every rotation. The cure for the problem is, firstly, to remove any twist already present in the fly line by the use of a line twist remover (as described in Chapter 2), and then to ensure that the problem does not happen again. This is achieved by ensuring that the rod moves in a straight backward and forward plane during false casting, and by making sure that the weight forward rear taper does not extend outside the rod tip during the casting cycle. Marking the line as described below helps prevent this.

Casting should be easy and effortless, and it should be a pleasure to perform, which it is if done correctly. It should not be a struggle, or else the day will become a tiring and unsatisfying one. If casting is difficult and exhausting, it is probably due to a fault in technique.

Marking the Line

It is a good idea to take the rod and line to the park and go through the casting strokes, letting out greater and lesser lengths of line, to ascertain the optimum amount of line that needs to be aerialized to give maximum casting distance. When this point is reached, you will find that casting has a sweetness that is not present when the rod is underloaded with not enough line out and you have to work hard to keep the momentum going, or when it is overloaded with too much line out and all becomes heavy and sloppy.

When the optimum has been satisfactorily established, mark the line over a length of 6in with a felt-tip marker between the reel and the butt ring, so that during fishing the correct amount of line, and no more and no less, is aerialized before line shoot. I also like to mark my lines with a different colour 5yd from the tip so that it is possible to judge when to start the hang or the lift off, with sufficient line outside the tip ring to load the rod sufficiently to make casting easy.

We all probably make one false cast too many from time to time, thereby wasting energy, wasting fishing time and making extra line flash, which can scare the fish, when one less would give better distance into the bargain. Take a look at other anglers' rods and lines when they are casting in the sunshine and you will see how they flash as they catch and reflect the sun. The trout must surely be suspicious of such an unnatural phenomenon and it could well make them more wary or nervous, if not actually putting them down.

Takes Occur at Longer Range

Consistent casting brings with it an extra benefit, which is perhaps not always recognized fully. It is probably true to say that the vast majority of takes occur at or around our individual maximum casting range, whatever that happens to be, and there is a rational explanation for this. If we perform one of our longer casts and the fly line lands heavily and it disturbs the fish underneath and in the vicinity of it, if our next cast is 6yd shorter we will be placing the flies in what we could describe as 'disturbed water'. We know that disturbed fish are wary and suspicious and even if they do not swim away in alarm they do not take. Fishing out that particular cast could be a waste of time. On the other hand, by casting consistent distances the flies will land in water where the leader may have landed on previous casts, but not the heavier fly line. This must improve our chances and experience tends to bear this out.

This is another reason why it is prudent to fan the casts when fishing from the bank or from an anchored boat – so that the flies are always exploring new and undisturbed territory. When drifting in a boat this phenomenon does not occur, as the drift ensures that each successive cast is made into virgin water, and it must be one of the reasons why the method can be so successful when conditions for drifting are favourable.

Casting Sinking Lines

A word of caution: never attempt to start to cast a sunken line until it has firstly been retrieved and brought to the surface and is then laying on top of it. The roll cast is the method of doing this safely, once the start of the belly is well inside the tip ring, without damaging or breaking the rod.

Similarly, never try to start casting a floater with a full length of fly line out: it will only overload the rod. If it is necessary to lift off to present quickly to a rising fish, do it firmly but nevertheless gently. If it won't lift, the only alternative is to draw line until the start of the belly is again inside the tip ring. You will lose time, and you may well lose the fish, but better that than breaking an expensive rod.

Professional Tuition

Professional tuition is always a good idea and learning under the supervision of a qualified casting instructor is by far the best way of becoming proficient. Employing an APGAI or STANIC approved casting instructor will ensure that good technique is taught from the start.

From there on the advice would be to practise, practise, and practise even more until the skills become finely honed and what is described as 'muscle memory' kicks in. It may take three or four seasons before things come as second nature and casting can be done without consciously thinking about it, but rest assured that stage *will* eventually come.

Once the skills have been learned, it is still a good idea to have one's style checked from time to time, either by critically going through the basics oneself, or better still under the scrutiny of an instructor, to ensure that no bad habits have crept in.

This is not a work on casting, which is a complete subject in itself, but if the reader wishes to take the matter of casting further, the book on casting by Peter Mackenzie-Philps and the DVD by Michael Evans listed in the bibliography are both recommended.

5   Terminal Tackle, Leader Materials and Knots

Terminal tackle, which for the sake of clarity we will define as everything between the tip of the fly line and the knot that finally attaches the fly on the end, is such an important subject that it deserves a chapter of its own. How the terminal tackle is made up determines how the fly will be presented, and how the fly is presented can make all the difference between the trout accepting it or rejecting it. It is as important as that. It is much more than simply attaching a length of nylon to the end of the fly line and tying on a fly.

To return to basics, well-constructed terminal tackle is comprised of three elements:

1   The braided loop.
2   A braided leader or polymer leader.
3   A monofilament leader (or tippet) with or without droppers attached.

The permutations in the length and density of the braided or polymer leader, and the length, material, colour, diameter, breaking strain, and the number and spacing of the droppers (if any) of the monofilament leader are endless, but how these are constructed can often make the difference between a good bag, a poor one, or perhaps even a blank day. Each of the three component parts will be looked at in turn.

Correct method of loop to loop connection.

Braided Loops

The braided loop is in essence exactly what it sounds like: it is a section of braided material that is attached to the tip of the fly line with a loop incorporated at the end. In spite of its simplicity, it is essential for easily attaching and removing the rest of the terminal tackle without resorting to knots that take time to tie, introduce weakness, and eventually lead to them getting shorter and shorter.

The loop to loop method of joining different materials is a simple innovation and, provided it is done correctly, it will enable the component parts to sit together snugly without any weakness, yet slide apart easily when a change is needed. There is a right and a wrong way of doing things, and if it is done properly there will be no problems with the materials jamming together.

To remember the correct way of connecting the two loops together try remembering the acrostic 'ELSE':

E = The loop at the **E**nd of the fly line.
L = The **L**arge diameter loop of the braided or polymer leader.
S = The **S**mall diameter loop of the braided or polymer leader.
E = The loop at the **E**nd of the fly line.

The connection is done in three stages:

1   Put the loop at the End of the fly line through the Large diameter loop of the braided or polymer leader and slide the leader away up the fly line.
2   Put the Small diameter loop of the braided or polymer leader through the loop at the End of the fly line.
3   Pull it right through until the two loops come together and fit snugly and

tightly, but will also push apart quite easily when it is time to separate them again.

If they are put together the wrong way they will only jam and become difficult to part, and the loops will become kinked and distorted. Just remember 'ELSE'!

Braided Leaders and Polymer Leaders

The introduction of these extensions to the end of the fly line has had a profound effect on the fly fishing scene and, although the idea is simple, their invention can be described as truly revolutionary. The concept was to

Ravensthorpe Reservoir in Northamptonshire, completed in 1890. Many pioneers of modern stillwater fly fishing learnt their skills at this picturesque water.

introduce a tapered extension to the end of the fly line so that the energy of the cast could be transmitted right along the leader down to the fly and result in perfect turn-over, leaving everything in a straight line between the angler and the fly.

One of the things the early pioneers of stillwater fly fishing discovered was that the further away from the fly line the artificial fly was, the less wary the fish became. As a result longer and longer nylon leaders became the fashion, sometimes up to 25ft and longer, and simultaneously catches became larger and larger. The downside to all this, and there always is a downside, was that getting 25ft of nylon leader to lie in a straight line at the end of the cast was almost impossible.

These fly line extensions solved the problem to a great degree but also brought an extra bonus – that of varying the sinking rate by using different densities of material. Now we have numerous sink rates varying from floaters, intermediates, slow sinkers, right through to very fast sinkers. They generally come in lengths from 5ft to 10ft, with the shorter lengths being the most popular; longer lengths are utilized when the fish are very shy or the water is of exceptional clarity. These will cover all the requirements of the reservoir fly fisherman, whether he is fishing dry flies on the surface or, at the other extreme, employing deep fished boobies or nymphs right on the bottom in deep water.

Monofilament Leaders (or Tippets)

At first thought we would probably say that the purpose of the monofilament leader is solely to deceive the trout into thinking that the fly is not attached to anything else so it will take it oblivious of any deception. Whilst this is undoubtedly true, it is only one part of the story. It is also the means that allows us to present and work the fly in the manner that we have decided to be the most profitable. A free-falling fly may be taken by the fish, but one that is worked in such a way that its movement mimics that of the natural more closely, or is appealing in some other way, is far more likely to deceive the trout.

Nylon and fluorocarbon are the only materials used by trout anglers for leaders these days, and they are available in standard unstretched form, copolymer or, alternatively, in low-diameter material that has been pre-stretched or treated in some way. Each material has its own advantages and disadvantages, which are summarized in the table below.

It is up to the individual to decide which material to use, but for practically

Comparison of properties of leader materials

Material	Advantages	Disadvantages
Standard nylon	Cheap Wide range of knots possible Buoyancy for dry fly fishing	Larger diameter Generally coloured
Copolymer nylon and low-diameter nylon	Thinner than standard nylon Buoyancy for dry fly fishing	More expensive Limited range of knots can be used
Fluorocarbon (standard and low-diameter)	Less visible in water Less likely to tangle Sinks more easily	Even more expensive Limited range of knots can be used

The visibility of 6lb BS leader materials: copolymer 0.185mm diameter nylon (top), standard 0.22mm diameter fluorocarbon (centre), and standard 0.25mm diameter nylon (bottom). The materials were photographed out of the water (left) and beneath the water (right) at the same magnification. The reader can draw his own conclusions whether fluorocarbon is less visible.

all situations, apart from the use of nylon for dry fly rigs, the author wholeheartedly recommends fluorocarbon on account of its lack of visibility under water. The advantages it offers far outweigh any negative qualities and these days, for the sake of uniformity, he uses virtually nothing else.

The importance of having leaders that will not give way at the moment of testing is of such paramount importance that the author discards his used leader at the end of every outing. This ensures that any kinked, sun-affected, or otherwise damaged material is never going to be a problem. It only takes a few minutes to tie up a new leader after each fishing trip and it is well worth the small amount of time spent. It may put up the cost of leaders further, but compared to virtually every other piece of tackle, leader material is really very cheap. Many of the angling mail-order catalogues regularly have offers of 'buy one get one free' in respect of fluorocarbon, so it is wise to take advantage of these and stock up

with several spools at a time. The author generally gets through three or four 100yd spools of fluorocarbon in a season at a cost of around £20. Not a prohibitive amount surely?

Six Useful Knots for the Fly Fisherman

There are six basic knots that will serve all the purposes of the fly fisher. They are ones that he should get to know thoroughly and that are suitable for all the materials likely to be used.

At this point it is perhaps appropriate to mention a product by Loon called UV Knot Sense, which can be applied to nail knots, needle knots and the braided loop joint to smooth out any unevenness. It is simply applied and smoothed on, and then subsequently exposed to sunlight or alternatively to the light from a special UV torch to effect curing. It produces a smooth

Useful knots for the fly angler

Knot	Purpose

Bankside knots

Two-turn overhand loop knot — For making loops in monofilament.

An easily tied and very strong knot for forming leader loops.

Three-turn water knot — For tying droppers.

A useful knot for joining two lengths of nylon and for forming droppers. When used for droppers it is important to use the strand pointing away from the fly line as it is the strongest one. Using the upper strand exposes a weakness due to the acute angle formed when the knot is put under tension.

Tucked four-turn half-blood knot — For attaching the fly to the leader.

This knot is almost unbeatable. Four turns is the right number, any less and there is a possibility of slipping, any more and friction causes the nylon to be hindered from pulling through smoothly. It is important to tuck the loose end through the final loop before pulling tight.

Knots for tackle preparation

Reel end (or arbor) knot — For attaching backing to the reel spool.

A few turns of backing wound on top of itself will enable the backing to grip the spool and stop it slipping.

Six-turn nail knot (or the similar needle knot) — For attaching backing to the end of the fly line.

Six turns around the fly line is about the correct number. The knot should be tightened so that the backing beds nicely into the fly line. Also used for attaching a thick piece of nylon to the end of the fly line if braided or polymer leaders are not used.

Braided loop joint — For attaching a braided loop to the end of the fly line (not actually a knot but included here for completeness).

Mastering the method of attaching a braided loop is necessary. It is straightforward but does take time and care to do properly.

joint that will pass through the rod tip ring without snagging.

Knots are Important

For many anglers the subject of fishing knots is either one that is confusing due to its complexity, or else something that is given far too little care and thought – the latter approach usually being accompanied at some point by disastrous results and loud groans. Getting to know which knots to use, and then learning to tie them properly, takes a little time but it is well worth the effort. *Knots really are important!* They are the weakest point in the many links between

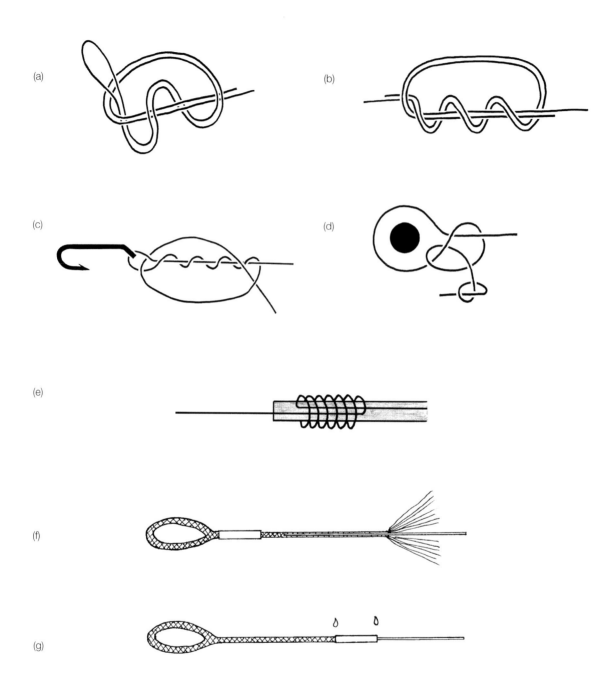

Illustrations of recommended knots. (a) Two-turn overhand loop knot. (b) Three-turn water knot. (c) Tucked four-turn half-blood knot. (d) Reel end knot. (e) Six-turn nail knot. (f) Braided loop joint, step 1. (g) Braided loop joint, step 2.

One that didn't get away! A 9lb 12oz rainbow caught by Robert Huggett of Leicester from Rutland Water in 1991 on a tandem Appetiser. Every fly angler dreams about landing a glass-case fish.

angler and fish, and it is therefore essential to understand our knots as best we can.

Fish can come unstuck for a variety of reasons, but probably the most disappointing one is when the knot fails, because that is something that *can* be prevented in the majority of cases. We have all heard stories of the fish breaking the line and as a result the 'fish of the season' making its escape. We should therefore give the matter some very careful thought. It is generally the knots in monofilament that are the cause of all the trouble and so they need the closest attention.

Nylon and fluorocarbon are wonderful materials and a real boon to the fly fisherman, being such a vast improvement on any of the materials that our forefathers used; but they do need treating with respect if they are to be utilized to their full potential. They should be our ally, not something to be treated with suspicion and which we suspect will let us down at the crucial moment.

There are no marks to be gained for well-tied knots (although there will definitely be some extra fish in the bag) but there are a lot of tears (and a lot of 'fish that got away' stories) as a result of badly tied ones!

Reasons for Knot Failure

Assuming that the line has not got any manufacturing defects, the main reasons why the leader parts company with the fish can be summarized as follows:

- The line is too weak for its purpose because too light a breaking strain has been chosen.
- The line has deteriorated, or has become damaged or frayed in some way.
- The line has been broken by a snatch or a smash take.
- The strike was too severe.
- An incorrect knot for the job in hand has been chosen.
- The knot has been poorly formed.
- The knot has not been correctly lubricated.
- The knot has not been drawn together correctly or tightly enough.
- The knot has been over-tightened.
- The knot has come undone for whatever reason.
- The difference in diameter between two different strands was too great.
- Joining dissimilar leader materials has been attempted (joining different

materials or any of the nylons to fluorocarbon should not be attempted).

It is up to each individual to decide on the correct balance between having the line strong enough for its purpose and not having it too conspicuous to spook the fish unnecessarily and thereby reduce the number of takes. Different leader materials of the same breaking strain can vary significantly in diameter and the table below shows that taking time choosing which one to use is a profitable exercise.

Although they all have the same breaking strain, the thinnest material is 56 per cent smaller in diameter compared to the thickest. To balance that it is necessary to remind ourselves that it was also around five times more expensive than the cheapest.

It is important to understand that these materials can deteriorate with age and so they should be stored out of the light and in cool conditions. It is a good idea to be ruthless and dispose of any leader material that is old (two or three seasons old in the case of the lowest breaking strains) or is in any way suspect. It is cheap enough in comparison with other items of tackle, and to use a fresh leader for each new fishing trip is a sound policy.

It is a good idea to buy leader materials from a retailer who can be relied on to have a fast stock turnover, rather than a smaller outlet that may have old material

Comparison of diameter of 6lb BS leader materials

Leader material	Typical diameter ranges (mm)
Standard nylon	0.22–0.25
Copolymer nylon	0.17–0.20
Low-diameter nylon	0.18–0.19
Standard fluorocarbon	0.20–0.24
Low-diameter fluorocarbon	0.16–0.18

on the shelf. Avoid anywhere that has its nylon hanging up in sunlight where UV rays can quickly weaken it. It is said that fluorocarbon is immune to UV light, but I take no chances and keep it away from the light as well.

There is little doubt that knots do seem to become stronger and better with the practice of repeated tyings and it is therefore wise for the angler to take care in the knots that he initially chooses, that he learns to tie them well, and that he does not chop and change them without very good reason.

For the reservoir angler, the six knots that have been described will cover all his needs and they can be recommended with confidence. They can be used with standard nylon and also with fluorocarbon, copolymer and low-diameter pre-stretched materials that do not accept strangulation knots well. They are all relatively easy to tie and a couple of hours and a spool of old nylon, practising them over and over again, is all that should be required to be conversant with them. No specialist tools are required except perhaps a nail or large needle in the case of the knots that bear their names. The time spent practising these knots at home will be amply rewarded on the bank.

It can be quite enlightening to subject these trial tyings to close scrutiny under a magnifying glass, as this will bring to light any errors (and perhaps a few horrors) that cannot be detected by a cursory glance with the naked eye. It will certainly concentrate the mind on getting them right.

Forming Knots Correctly

It is important when forming knots to ensure that the turns are laying correctly alongside each other and that they are not out of line in a manner that allows them to cut into one another once the knot is drawn tight. If, during the initial formation of the turns, it is found that they are incorrect or out of line, the best policy is to undo the whole thing and start all over again. If this is not done, the fish will almost certainly exploit any weaknesses!

The number of turns necessary for each knot is dependent on the surface finish, diameter, elasticity and strength of the material being used, and a few trials will quickly determine the correct number for each knot/material combination.

It is essential that all knots are well lubricated before pulling tight, either with spit or with one of the special products made for the purpose, as this eliminates the material being over-stretched or overheating and becoming damaged. Knots that are formed properly do not need the additional security of the application of superglue.

Knots should be drawn together smoothly and steadily, pulling on all the ends evenly to ensure that the turns bed down snugly. Whatever happens, never pull the strands together with a jerk, as this will only weaken the knot. Do not over-tighten the knot, as this again will only weaken it. Experience will show when a knot has been drawn to its optimum tightness, and that is where practice in tying and then subsequently testing knots to destruction teaches a great deal.

When tying on a new fly it is as well not to trim the monofil too closely but to leave

a stub of around a millimetre or so to allow for a minimal amount of slippage in the eventuality of a strong pull.

Retie if Necessary

If the knot is not 100 per cent correct, the best thing to do is to cut it off and start afresh. It may be a nuisance, but the trouble will be amply repaid.

I am sure we have all experienced those occasions at one time or another when we have examined our leader to find that although we may have felt little or nothing, one of our flies has simply gone and all that remains is a curly end. That could well be the result of a smash take where the fish has snatched against the drag of the fly line.

It should be remembered that although the advent of low stretch fly lines has paid dividends in terms of increased bite detection and hooking properties, the downside of this benefit is that their elasticity and shock absorption are much reduced, thus putting extra strain on the leader. Nylon and fluorocarbon are materials that have great strength when subjected to gradual increases in pressure, but much less so when the increase is sudden, and smash takes can test knots beyond the limits of their endurance. Try this simple experiment of tying

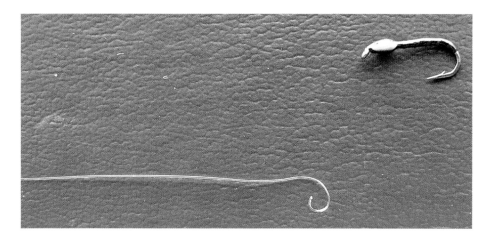

The result of a smash take.

49

a length of material with a loop on either end: firstly, pull it slowly apart to break it, and then jerk it quickly. You will probably be surprised at how strong it is when the pressure is built up slowly and yet how easily it breaks with the jerk.

The 'give' of braided and polymer leaders can help cushion shocks to some extent, but they are not to be considered as a complete answer to the problem. It is therefore vitally important to take care in tying, and to use the spring of the rod, by holding it at a slight angle to the line when retrieving quickly, to help avoid disappointments.

It is wise to check knots occasionally during fishing in case any have become loose. They can then be drawn up tightly again or re-tied. It is also vital to check leaders for necking loops or wind knots (caused during casting rather than by the wind, but it is convenient to blame something else!) regularly as these reduce the breaking strain considerably (by over 50 per cent). If one is detected, undo it at once by pushing a pin through it and open it out. If a wind knot is so tight that it is impossible to untie it, cut the line and tie it together again using a water knot.

When there are troubles it is almost invariably the knot that fails as opposed to a straight unknotted length of nylon, and that should concentrate our minds on the importance of the subject in hand. With time and practice the knots outlined in this chapter will become second nature, and it will be possible to tie them almost unconsciously and in very little time at all. As with all things 'fly fishing', it is important to take pains with every single aspect of tackle, as it is the little things that often make the difference between success and failure. Knots are no different.

We all have our own little quirks that we employ where knots are concerned, and it is up to each of us to find the way that works best for us as individuals. By doing things the most comfortable way we must surely make fewer mistakes and end up with more secure knots (and fish) in the process. The same holds good with the materials we use, and the ones in which we have the most confidence are invariably the ones that bring greater success out on the water.

Leader Design

How our leaders are designed and made up contributes to success, or the lack of it, more than we perhaps imagine. Leader design and fly presentation will be covered in detail in Chapter 7.

Three wet fly leaders of the required breaking strain are usually taken on each fishing trip, each loosely wound on a separate cast carrier to avoid memory coils. They are tied up carefully at home where the length and spacing of the droppers can be measured accurately (I have rule markings on the fly-tying bench where this is done) and the knots can be well lubricated and tightened properly and carefully. If a tangle is excessive the leader is removed and a new one

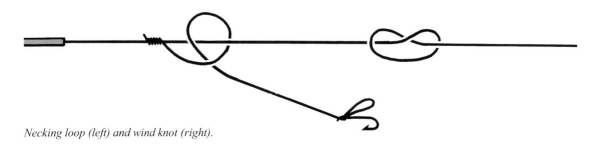

Necking loop (left) and wind knot (right).

Leader materials and applications

Material	Approx diameter (mm)	Application
Standard 6lb BS fluorocarbon	0.22	General use
Standard 8lb BS fluorocarbon	0.25	Heavier fish and boobies
Standard 10lb BS fluorocarbon	0.28	Muddler stripping and 'Northampton' style
Low-diameter 6lb BS fluorocarbon	0.18	Extra clear conditions
Copolymer 6lb BS nylon	0.185	Dry fly fishing

is tied on to replace it. I cannot remember getting through more than three in any one fishing trip in recent years and generally just one or two, depending on the number of rods that are set up, is sufficient.

It is not so easy to perform the task of tying up leaders out on the bank; the wind may be blowing the leader around, measuring lengths of material is not so easy, stopping them all blowing away can be a serious problem, and on top of that we are perhaps over eager to hurry things and start fishing. Why waste valuable fishing time doing something that can be done far better and more quickly at home?

All other leaders, which are simpler and less trouble to tie, are made up at the waterside as tactics dictate.

Breaking Strain

Generally, the use of standard 6lb BS (0.22mm diameter) fluorocarbon would cover most requirements in the Midlands reservoirs, and I would be more than happy to play a double figure fish on a 6lb BS tippet. It would be more likely for the hook to pull out or straighten than for the fluorocarbon to break. Breaks generally occur on the take and not whilst a fish is being played. Incidentally, the 7lb 8oz rainbow shown on the frontispiece was taken on 6lb BS fluorocarbon and a size 12 Kamasan B400 emerger hook.

When extra large fish are expected I would possibly consider going up to 8lb BS (0.25mm diameter) fluorocarbon, although in truth, apart from boobies, muddler stripping and 'Northampton' style fishing, I have not used 8lb or 10lb BS material for the past three seasons.

Should conditions dictate that something finer than standard 6lb BS material be used, I might consider using one of the low-diameter fluorocarbons of 0.18mm diameter; this is thinner than standard material but still has a breaking strain of 6lb.

The range of leader materials above should be sufficient to cope with most situations likely to be encountered.

6 A Reasoned Approach to Fly Choice

The choice of which flies to use in any given situation is something that many anglers find bewildering; and yet in order to improve catch rates it is necessary to formulate a reasoned approach to fly choice that is based on sound thinking, logic and experience, rather than mere random selection. If there are valid reasons why one fly is preferred over another, it does at least form the basis of a strategy that can be developed and modified in the light of experience, whether successful or not; a lucky dip approach, on the other hand, will provide no logical foundation upon which to build.

To arrive at a rational approach, it is essential that things are always considered from the trout's point of view and what they want, not from the angler's and what he would like to give them. It is also vital to be versatile and to have a wide range of tactics, ones with which we are fully conversant, available at our fingertips and not be afraid to change and modify them continually until the successful method of the day has been found. Sticking to a standardized approach, which is employed every time without any thought to the prevailing conditions, may catch a few fish on occasion, but it will never produce results on a consistent basis in a wide range of conditions.

The Trout

The trout is a carnivorous feeder and a very catholic one in its tastes. Its feeding habits can vary greatly, from gently cruising around and delicately sipping in tiny morsels, to attacking and devouring its prey with a savage ferocity that can sometimes beggar belief.

The behaviour of a single fish can vary from day to day, and indeed it can shift from one feeding pattern to another during the course of the same day, and then back again. Moreover, to complicate matters further, not every fish will be acting in the same manner at the same moment in time. Nevertheless, to be successful the angler has to decide what the majority of the trout within his casting compass want at any given moment, and attempt to give them something that they will find appealing in both form and movement.

Like any other hunter of wild game, the fly fisher needs to have a good understanding of how his quarry behaves, how it reacts to stimuli, and how the prevailing conditions affect it. Our knowledge is limited and what we know has to be gleaned from scientific data and from fishing experience. Trout possess eyes, internal 'ears', nostrils and mouths and it is probable that their senses operate much like those of humans.

Sight

Trout largely hunt by sight and have very keen vision, which is in colour in normal light levels and monochrome at low light levels, like man, although it is possible that they may see more or less of the colour spectrum. They are not colour blind! In deep water where little light penetrates and where divers are able to see very little, trout are able to see and take their prey quite readily.

Touch

Trout are curious fish. Having no hands or fingers to feel and explore things they use their mouths instead to test their food to see if it is edible, very often taking it into their mouths and spitting it out again several times. As noted elsewhere, they do ingest quite inedible items on occasion.

Sound

The underwater environment that trout inhabit is a silent one and most freshwater aquatic creatures make no sound whatsoever. However, the fish can and do detect vibrations from both within the water and outside it, which they pick up along their lateral line. The avoidance of dropping things in the boat and banging about on the bank is therefore important.

Taste

Trout swallow their food whole rather than chew it and so it would seem that taste is not particularly important; yet there is the paradox that trout eat most of the food items readily available to them but ignore a few creatures such as silverhorn sedges, alder flies and some aquatic beetles on a consistent and presumably selective basis. Why this should be is a mystery.

Smell

Trout do have nostrils and are able to detect odours, but apart from those times when they are rooting about on the bottom, most of their prey is engulfed and devoured at speed and so its smell would seem to be of little importance. It is probable that this sense is not as well developed in trout (which are carnivorous) as it is in coarse fish (which are largely omnivorous). Coarse anglers use aromatic ingredients in baits and ground bait to attract fish, but attempts to produce similar attractants for trout have, by and large, proved to make little difference.

Intelligence

How intelligent trout are is a matter of conjecture and has been the subject of debate by anglers for generations. In truth, although the trout is an unreasoning and often illogical creature, which is driven by the need to feed and reproduce, it is also vigilant, wary and has a limited ability to remember and learn from experience. On one hand, we can credit trout with an almost supernatural intelligence and, on the other, assume that it has no brainpower whatsoever. To be on the safe side, it is probably best to assume that our quarry is more intelligent and cautious than it really is rather than the reverse. We underestimate them at the risk of much reduced catches.

Pain

It is inconceivable that trout experience pain in the same way as human beings. In spite of savage wounds inflicted by cormorants, pike, mink and other predators, trout appear to swim around and feed quite normally. Our understanding of the nervous system of trout would appear to be very limited.

Probably the most destructive creature to afflict and decimate our inland waterways and fisheries – the dreaded cormorant contemplating his next meal!

Trout do not experience pain in the same way as humans. In spite of horrendous wounds this rainbow was feeding normally. It took a Rough GRHE cast into the ring of a rise.

Browns and Rainbows

Brown and rainbow trout have similar feeding habits, and although the vast majority of trout caught will probably be rainbows, the tactics discussed in this book are applicable to both species. Browns are stocked less frequently nowadays as a result of their slower growth rate and hence greater cost per fish, but they will turn up from time to time (providing they are stocked!). Rainbows are more of a shoaling fish than browns, which tend to acquire more solitary habits as they get older, but otherwise the behaviour of both is much alike and for our purposes the two species will be treated as one.

Fly Choice

There are three main approaches to fly choice that can be adopted, and flies that have been designed to suit each particular one, in an effort to deceive the fish. They can be broadly summarized as offering the fish an artificial fly that is one of the following:

1   A close copy '*exact imitation*' of a natural food form that the trout are known or expected to be taking. Examples of such flies would include the Blakestone Buzzer, Living Damsel and Peeping Caddis.

2   A '*suggestive deceiver*' incorporating features of recognition: either of a natural food form that the trout are known or expected to be taking, or else something that the trout could perceive to be a source of food. It could be described as a 'calculated suggestion'. Typical examples are the Gold Ribbed Hare's Ear, Pheasant Tail Nymph and my Olive Grizzle Palmer. Patterns such as the Dawson's Olive, Black & Green Marabou and Tadpole

A well-conditioned rainbow trout. Rainbows are by far the most common trout in reservoirs; they feed in a wider range of conditions; they fight better; and arguably they taste better as well!

A brownie from Rutland Water. The native brown trout is a very striking fish and holds a place of special admiration and respect in the heart of every fly angler.

The capture of a superb 2lb 4oz blue trout like this is what fly fishing is all about. It may not be huge – but it is a beautiful and hard-fighting fish.

can be fished as deceivers when retrieved slowly so that they move in a lifelike manner.

3   A '*lure*' (attractor or flasher) that the fish will take as a result of either its in-built curiosity or its aggression, rather than in expectation of it being food. Flies such as the Cat's Whisker and Tadpole will be retrieved more quickly with pauses between the pulls to allow the mobile materials to work in the water. As an alternative, brightly coloured flashers can be employed and these are normally retrieved at much faster speeds.

In a sport like ours, which has so many variables, and with a fickle fish like the trout to complicate matters even further, these approaches often overlap with blurred edges, so that one method will encroach upon another depending, firstly, on the flies selected and, secondly, on how they are fished. Nevertheless, in order to clarify things, it is probably best to consider each of these three primary alternatives as a separate rationale.

Deciding on which approach is adopted, what fly it is decided to tie on the leader, and how it is subsequently fished, will crystallize the angler's whole philosophy of trout fishing.

The versatile angler will at different times utilize all three approaches as the conditions and the fish dictate. It is suggested, however, that the use of suggestive deceivers will, in the majority of circumstances, result in the most consistent bags. This may sound a sweeping statement, but it is one that is made and has been proved to be correct time and time again as a result of fishing experiences, the recording of catches (and the lack of them as well) and a good deal of thought. Any theories that have not been proved out on the reservoir bank in fishing conditions are speculation, and ultimately worthless and unhelpful, however plausible they may appear in the abstract.

The three alternative approaches will now be examined in turn.

Exact Imitations

In theory, offering the trout an exact copy of what it is feeding on at the time would appear to be the ideal solution to tempt them to take our offerings. If it is feeding on a particular food item, then a close copy imitation must surely be taken as well. It seems plausible, but unfortunately there are several drawbacks to what is in effect, once things have been carefully thought through, an oversimplistic approach.

Firstly, although we can produce fly patterns that at first glance may appear to look very much like the naturals, when they are examined with a critical eye they do fall short in many areas: in colour, transparency, delicacy and so on. In addition, by being lifeless in themselves they cannot possibly have that vital in-built movement and animation that natural creatures possess.

Secondly, we have to ask ourselves if it is possible, when drawing a fly through the water 25yd away, to move it in a way that exactly mimics the movement of a living creature, with its often eccentric jerky darting back and forth. Watching natural creatures moving around in the margins shows us that this movement is difficult to replicate. We try our hardest, but at best can only perform a rough approximation.

Thirdly, fishing experience shows that on many occasions trout swallow an artificial that is very different to the food they are taking. To substantiate this assertion we will look at four autopsies from the author's fishing records. They illustrate that these particular trout preferred flies that bore little resemblance to the food they were taking:

1   Eyebrook Reservoir, bank fishing in May: after previous very heavy rain the water was coloured and at maximum level in the margins. A rainbow trout of 1lb 7oz was found to be full of earth-worms and a few caddis larvae. The fish was taken on a Black & Green Holographic Buzzer. (*See* spooning illustrated in Chapter 9.)

2   Ringstead Grange Fishery, boat fishing in June: air full of adult damsels. Autopsies showed that the fish were largely feeding on damsel larvae. Six fish caught: they were taken on Black & Red Holographic Buzzer (3), Black & Green Holographic Buzzer (1), Dawson's Olive (1) (a damsel sugges-tion?) and an Olive Grizzle Palmer (1) (ditto?).

3   Thornton Reservoir, boat fishing in May: trout caught had live black and silver buzzer pupae in its stomach, proving that they had only been eaten minutes before. Despite a Black & Sil-ver Holographic Buzzer being on the next dropper, the trout took a Silver Spider instead – a suggestive black and silver pattern.

4   Thornton Reservoir, boat fishing in mid October: limit taken in under 3 hr. None of the fish had any significant food in their stomachs. Seven were

The limit bag of Thornton trout. None of the fish had much food in their stomach.

taken on a Black & Green Marabou and one on a mini Cat's Whisker; both fished deep and slow on an intermediate line. Autopsies of the eight fish were as follows:

Fish 1: weed.
Fish 2: few pieces of weed.
Fish 3: a 2in long twig.
Fish 4: few tiny mites.
Fish 5: two tiny beetles.
Fish 6: weed, a few daphnia, one feather.
Fish 7: one buzzer pupa, a few daphnia.
Fish 8: completely empty.

The conclusion from these observations must be that creating lifelike imitations is difficult, as is moving them in a lifelike way – and frequently it does not matter anyway! Fly fishing is not an exact science, but how many times have two flies been fished on the same leader, one of which could be called a reasonably close copy of what is later found to be in the fish's stomach, and the other a mere suggestive deceiver of food in general, and the trout took the latter?

Suggestive Deceivers

The second alternative is to offer the trout impressionist fly patterns that are designed to roughly replicate and mimic food forms that the fish will recognize in very general terms.

Although they are not what would be called close copy imitations, they will incorporate some of the features that the fish would normally expect to find in the underwater creatures that are their prey – features such as size and coloration, tapered bodies, bulky thoraces, legs represented by hackles, fine tails, segmented bodies, movement (obtained by the use of very mobile materials such as marabou),

trapped air in their bodies (imitated by the judicious use of tinsel), and so on. These features are what are called recognition points, and a few of them incorporated into a single pattern seem to satisfy the trout that they are indeed food and are to be taken without hesitation. Very often these features are exaggerated in size, colour or effect, and this exaggeration seems to enhance their attractiveness and effectiveness rather than diminish it. In addition to size, shape and coloration, when they are fished in a manner that the fish would expect its natural prey to adopt, and generally this is slow and/or jerky in its overall movement, then the deception hopefully becomes complete, or certainly complete enough to satisfy the fish. One of the reasons for the success of suggestive deceivers would seem to be because the fish are looking for points of *recognition* rather than points of *difference*.

Fishing with suggestive deceivers is a straightforward approach, but like all things nothing is ever quite as simple as it might appear. It is much more than merely choosing a good all-round deceiver pattern such as a hare's ear nymph, tying three of them on to the leader, and then fishing

An artificial and a natural buzzer pupa. An imitation as close as this generally satisfies the fish.

59

the same combination day in and day out throughout the season. There is (thankfully for the sport) no such thing as a killing fly that works in all circumstances.

Trout do have their preferences of fly, as even the most hidebound lure angler would readily agree, and they do have a partiality for a particular fly on one day, which will change for reasons we do not understand properly to a different fly on another day. It therefore stands to reason that possessing a selection of flies of different sizes, colours and shapes will be necessary, and that selecting the correct one from them is done for good reasons.

If artificial flies are utilized that possess some similar basic characteristics to the food the trout are taking or they might expect to find, and they are moved in a lifelike way, it will most likely increase the chances of success. The fish usually take such flies confidently, rather than merely pluck at them timidly as they sometimes do with lures, which can result in a lightly hooked fish that may eventually escape. In order to have the best chance of attracting the trout to our offerings it is important to know:

- What food the trout are taking or might expect to find at the time.
- What food form(s) each of the artificial flies employed probably represents (although each individual fly may represent more than one particular creature to the fish).

When both the above questions have been answered correctly, it is possible to make an informed decision of what fly to select, and then endeavour to employ it in a correspondingly lifelike manner.

Being able to identify the various creatures that trout feed on by performing autopsies on any fish that have been caught, and by careful observation of what is going on at the waterside, is consequently vital; Chapters 9 and 10 deal with these two fundamental and important disciplines.

Fishing from both the bank and the boats by many experienced and successful anglers, as well as the author, confirms that this approach does work, and that the trout take with an assurance that not only surprises the trout, but very often surprises the angler too!

One successful line of approach is to employ a Dawson's Olive, Tadpole or other deceiver constructed with marabou, soft hackles and other very flexible materials as a point fly, with smaller nymphs on the droppers. This arrangement enables the leader to turn over easily, keeps everything in a taut and straight line when retrieving, and using a weighted point fly enables the rig to fish more deeply if that is required. Life and movement are imparted when a slow figure of eight or perhaps a gently twitched retrieve is utilized in conjunction with the very mobile materials incorporated in the construction of the flies. The trout will be teased and tempted into taking and one can imagine such flies, fished so that they seem to breathe and pulsate with natural life, being drifted slowly across the fish's nose and being snapped up in an instinctive and involuntary reflex action. It may be pure speculation as to why and how it happens but the method does work, and takes are often firm and confident pulls. Such a line of attack as this shows the grey areas that clearly exist between the three fishing approaches.

Whether a fly/retrieve combination being fished is actually that of a deceiver or a lure is really a question of how these terms are defined. The author would define a deceiver as something that the trout will investigate to see if it is food, and a lure as something that the fish will investigate to see what it is. How the trout would define them is another matter and open to conjecture.

Lures (Attractors or Flashers)

There are times when appealing to the hunger of the trout is simply not productive because the fish are not feeding for whatever reason. When this is the case it is necessary to resort to provoking either their curiosity or their aggression to persuade them to take our offerings. This is done by using attractors fished much faster. The flies are cast out and then stripped back quite quickly, with variations in the rate of retrieve and the pauses in between in order to arouse the interest of the trout. Here the fish are offered only a brief look at the artificial in the hope that they will take instantly by a spontaneous and unconscious response. Flies such as the Cat's Whisker and Tadpole are suitable candidates for fishing in this manner.

This may be a rather repetitive way of fishing, with its continual casting out and stripping back, and it may not be to everyone's liking, but it is a valid (and legal) approach. In spite of the fact that there is no logical reason why flies fished at such speeds should be taken, they do catch trout at those times when the more imitative approaches are not profitable, and it is therefore unwise not to give them a try. Trout often mouth flies fished like this and then spit them out, often several times, before they are either hooked, become suspicious and drop them, or simply lose interest. On occasion they will follow the flies for a considerable distance without taking, often causing bow waves in the process, and they will only swirl away on approaching and seeing the angler.

As a further alternative, the use of brightly coloured and even gaudy flashers such as the Alexandra, Mickey Finn or Whiskey Fly can be employed. These flies bear no relationship to any natural item that the trout will encounter in the normal course of events, or anything that naturally swims in the water, but trout do take them. Flashers such as these are generally fished at much higher speeds than other attractors in an attempt to complete the deception.

Trout seem to have day-to-day preferences in the colour of lure that they find acceptable – black, white, orange/yellow and green/olive seem to be the most appealing – and it is therefore prudent to alternate the colours until the acceptable one is discovered.

Conclusions

These are the three alternative approaches from which a choice has to be made, but, as has already been stated, it is proposed that suggestive deceivers will be the best option most times (unless we have any firm guidance to the contrary) and results prove that they can be fished with every confidence.

Once the flies have been chosen it is then necessary to fish them in a manner that will deceive the fish. The way the flies behave in the water is dependent on leader design and this subject will be dealt with in the next chapter.

7 Leader Construction, Retrieve Methods and the 'Take'

The way that the flies are presented to the fish often makes all the difference between acceptance and refusal, and as leader (or tippet) design is all part of the deception it needs careful thought. It is therefore time to look into the various considerations that need to be taken into account when they are designed and tied up. They can be summarized as follows:

- The material should be as thin as possible to deceive the fish.
- The material should be as strong as possible for the fish it is hoped to catch.
- The material should be of as inconspicuous a colour as possible as the water colour dictates.
- Any leader shine should be removed with a sinking compound.
- The leader should be as long as can comfortably be cast (within reason).
- The leader should be easy to cast, and should turn over in a straight line.
- The leader should have as many droppers as possible to increase the chances of an appropriate fly being presented to the fish (many fisheries restrict the number of hooks to four, which for practical purposes is as many as will be needed).

- The number of droppers should be reduced in very clear water (because the visibility of more than one fly at a time to the fish appears to be detrimental) and also when fishing into a head wind (to avoid tangles).

The leaders discussed here are in addition to the braided or polymer leader of (usually) 5ft in length attached to the end of the fly line. Therefore, with a 16ft monofilament leader attached, the tail fly will, in actuality, be 21ft away from the tip of the fly line and the others in similar proportion. That is sufficient a distance, it is proposed, to fool the fish.

All other things being equal, employing long leaders will make a profound difference to the number of takes for obvious reasons – the flies are more distant from line splash, line shadow and line wake.

Leader Turnover and Keeping in Touch with the Flies

Casting the longer leaders recommended (and some anglers use leaders much longer than these) is not particularly difficult when using three or four flies increasing in size (and therefore weight) towards the point, as there will normally be sufficient momentum to enable the leader to turn over easily, providing the correct rod and line combination is being used. It is the weight of the flies rather than their size that is the significant factor, and chenille- and wool-bodied flies, which absorb large amounts of water, make casting much easier, but do not sink significantly quicker than other patterns as most of the mass is made up of water.

It is wise to watch the flies alight so that the angler can see (a) whether the leader has landed in a straight line and (b) if a tangle has occurred. If conditions are such that the leader does not turn over properly, the last few yards of fly line being shot on the final forward delivery stroke should be very gently feathered down to ensure that the flies arrive in a straight line. That way the flies will be fishing from the moment they touch down. There is a bonus in using a heavier point fly – it acts as an anchor for the leader, keeping everything much straighter and thus improving bite detection. Tapered leaders are an unnecessary luxury (and expense) and the ones that follow are all tied from a single diameter (and hence breaking strain) material.

Dropper Length

I like to use long droppers, of around 12in, for most leaders. This length keeps the flies well away from the main leader. If the dropper wraps round the main leader a few times, the fly itself will still be a fair distance away from it.

Tying on the first fly will lose an inch or so in length, and each subsequent tying will remove another inch or so each time. As each leader is discarded after every fishing trip, it is a rare occurrence for any dropper to become so short that it is not possible to tie on a new fly.

If circumstances should dictate that a shorter dropper is necessary, it is a simple matter to snip off a few inches and tie the fly on to the shortened dropper (as an example, when fishing loch style in light winds, a short dropper makes it possible to dibble the bob fly without a portion of leader material dragging along the surface with the fly, which might alarm the fish).

Leaders for Wet Fly Fishing

For simplicity the basic leader employed for the majority of wet fly work is shown below, and it is brought ready tied up from home.

When fishing into a headwind and a shorter leader is required, the top 30in, complete with the top dropper, is snipped off and a new loop is tied to give a two dropper leader of 13ft. This rig can also be used when there is no wind and casting is

2ft 6in   4ft   4ft   5ft 6in

Basic 16ft wet fly leader, with 3 × 12in droppers, in 6lb BS or 8lb BS fluorocarbon.

3ft 6in   4ft   5ft 6in

Leader reduced to 13ft, with 2 × 12in droppers, in 6lb BS or 8lb BS fluorocarbon.

more difficult and a team of small flies will not turn over easily on the 16ft leader.

If the water clarity is exceptional and the fish are shy, a 16ft leader is still used but this time with two droppers.

Other rigs that may be used are much simpler and they can easily and quickly be tied up at the waterside as required.

For static boobies the leader used is simply a short length of 8lb BS fluorocarbon of between 1ft and 3ft, with 18in generally being about the right length. If weeds are a problem it may be necessary to lengthen the leader to get above them and avoid snagging.

When 'back-drifting' a booby behind a drifting boat using an ultra fast sinking line, the length would be increased up to 8ft or more and a dropper can be incorporated if necessary to search more than one depth at a time.

For muddler stripping a 10ft leader is utilized, with or without a single dropper, this time in 10lb BS material.

These basic leaders should cover most eventualities, but with all things in fly fishing being so variable it is up to the angler to modify things as he sees fit so that fishing can be performed with confidence. It is a simple matter to lengthen or shorten leaders (at either end) if required. If what is being done does not inspire full confidence, then either change or modify it. Only by trial and error, and continually experimenting, will progress be made. It is all part of the process of developing into being a *thinking* fly angler.

Working the Flies: Methods of Retrieve

How the fly is retrieved in the water, and as a consequence whether or not it is moving in a manner that the trout considers to be attractive and lifelike, is one of the most crucial considerations, and it is just as important, and maybe even more important, than the choice of fly. Yet in spite of this how many times is the question asked, 'What fly did you catch on?' and how seldom, 'How was the fly being retrieved?'

Sixteen-foot leader for very clear water, with 2 × 12in droppers, in 6lb BS standard or low-diameter fluorocarbon.

Back-drifting leader up to 8ft, with 1 × 12in dropper (optional), in 8lb BS fluorocarbon.

Muddler leader of 10ft, with 1 × 12in dropper (optional), in 10lb BS fluorocarbon.

It is essential that the improving angler gets to know and use all the different methods of retrieve at their appropriate time, as on the day one particular style may well, and most probably will, outfish the others. Sticking to one method will only lead to limited success. The principal techniques of retrieving the flies are as follows:

On the drop

This is not a retrieve as such, but simply the pause after the fly has been delivered before it sinks to the desired depth. During such times it is important to keep in touch with the terminal tackle so that any pull or enquiry by the fish is registered, either by a visible movement of the fly line or alternatively by a pull to the hand.

The static retrieve

This leaves the fly stationary, or perhaps very nearly stationary, and only sufficient line is retrieved to keep in contact with the terminal tackle rather than move the fly. The classic use of this tactic is when a team of buzzer pupae or other nymphs are suspended just below the surface film, and the action of the wind on a (generally) floating fly line contributes the only movement necessary. In spite of its delicate presentation, takes can sometimes be arm-wrenchingly ferocious. Sometimes the fish will take a stationary fly when they will not look at a moving one.

The figure of eight

This classic nymph fisher's retrieve is to slowly, indeed sometimes exceedingly slowly, recover line in the hand by drawing it in with the finger and thumb and then pass it on to the other three fingers before taking another pull with the finger and thumb; and so on. The resultant coils that

have been retrieved are either dropped into a line tray or on to the floor of the boat. This retrieve moves the line in a steady and continuous manner.

The twitch

A variation on the figure of eight, but with quick and very jerky sharp pulls by the fingers interspersed between the continuous figure of eight retrieve. When fishing flies with a marabou wing or tail, a static booby, or a Flexi Bloodworm with its long Flexi-floss legs, this twitch imparts a lifelike and irresistible movement to the fly.

The slow draw

This is similar to the strip described below, but it is used with deceivers as opposed to lures. It is carried out more slowly, with variations in the speed of pull and with long or short pauses interspersed between the pulls.

The strip

This is accomplished by the left hand holding the line between finger and thumb at the butt ring and pulling steadily back as far as the arm will comfortably stretch. This can be slow, fast, or even very fast, as experience dictates on the day. When it is fished quickly it gives the fish a quick look at the fly in the hope that it will make a snap decision to take.

As with all the retrieves, the fish may mouth the fly several times. This results either in little plucks or perhaps what can best be described as a 'tactile rattle' being felt by the hand until the fish either decides to take properly or alternatively rejects the fly. When this occurs, keep on retrieving at the same speed until something happens. It doesn't always work and if the fish are continually plucking but not taking, some say speed up the fly, others say slow down, and still others say stop! Striking at such plucks does not usually result in the fish being hooked and so it is as well to wait for a definite pull before tightening.

The 'roly-poly'

This is the fastest of all the retrieves and is executed by tucking the rod under the armpit and drawing line quickly and continuously using each hand in turn. It is employed when the fish are in a chasing mood and can be used with a sunk fly, or alternatively a muddler or booby stripped along the surface. Takes are often dramatic, with the trout causing bow waves as they home in on the fly. Fish this method using stronger leaders than normal.

The dibble

When a bushy bob fly breaks the surface at the end of the retrieve it can be held dibbling in the surface film for some seconds, or alternatively slowly drawn over it causing a gentle wake. The fish sometimes find this action irresistible and it should regularly be employed both from the bank and the boat.

The hang

When fishing out a cast, at the very final moment of the retrieve, when the bob fly is dibbling on the surface and there is no more line to gather, it is wise to pause for a few seconds, or indeed many seconds, and wait. Trout that have followed, but not taken, will often take one of the flies, either during the hang or when the fly is moved once again as the line is slowly accelerated into the start of the next cast. Employing this tactic will put many more fish in the bag and on occasion the only sign there is of any fish being present is at this very final

stage. If a fish slashes as the flies are lifted off, immediately drop them back where they came from with a roll cast; the fish are often still looking round to find the fly, so give it to them.

It is important to vary the method of retrieve to ascertain the most successful taking method during successive casts, for example by employing a slow figure of eight interspersed with some pauses, twitches and faster pulls. Very often the fish will follow a fly for some time without taking, and only when the pattern of retrieve is varied in some way, either faster or slower, will they take. Whether this is a voluntary, involuntary or an induced response we do not know, but it works!

Dry Fly Fishing: Presenting a Static Fly

In spite of its increasing popularity nowadays, dry fly fishing is a relatively minor tactic on many reservoirs, and there are many days when it is a waste of time. That is not to say that it is completely useless, but that its use has to be carefully considered and employed when the conditions are right. To state the obvious, unless the fish are feeding at or close to the surface, if we are restricted to dries we will not be placing our offerings anywhere near them. Strange as it may seem, trout *will* take a dry fly when they are not visibly rising to the naturals. Perhaps if there are no naturals on the surface they have a choice of just one fly – ours!

When fishing dry flies or emergers, we are offering a motionless fly in the hope that the trout will see it and then take, and to do this it is necessary to ensure that the fish are not suspicious or alarmed. Good presentation is achieved, firstly, by making sure that the leader is sunk beneath the surface and is therefore less visible by

3ft   4ft   6ft

Dry fly leader of 13ft, with 2 × 12in droppers (optional), in 6lb BS copolymer nylon.

degreasing it regularly; and, secondly, by careful casting and subsequently gently feathering the line at the end of the cast so that the leader smoothly unfurls leaving the flies in a straight line.

As the flies are static, the trout have more time to inspect and reject them if they are not presented correctly. To ensure that the flies are sitting in the same manner as a natural, they need to be tied and then waterproofed so that they sit in, rather than on, the surface film to mimic hatching flies as they emerge and break through the surface. It is usually advantageous to clip any hackles on the underside of the fly parallel with the body so that the fly beds nicely into the surface film. The selective application of floatant to that part of the fly that is to be above the surface helps to achieve this aim. The basic dry fly leader is shown above.

Wet and Dry Fly Fishing

This might seem like a contradiction in terms, but fishing both wet and dry flies together can be a killing method when used at the appropriate time. There are two methods and they are both used with floating lines. When fish are taking flies on, actually in, or just under the surface film, is the time to employ them.

The first one, commonly called the 'washing line' method, consists of two buoyant flies, one at each end of the leader, with one or two wet patterns, usually holographic buzzers, diawl bachs, PTNs or similar nymphs strung out in between and held just below the surface film. The top dropper dry fly can be substituted with another nymph or emerger if required. The fish may take either the dry flies or the nymphs.

The second one, the 'suspended nymph' method, allows the wet flies to fish much deeper, and again consists of a buoyant bob fly; a deer hair or plastazote parachute emerger pattern has great buoyancy and is ideal for the purpose, with nymphs in the dropper and point positions.

Fished with the breeze gently drifting the flies round in an arc, takes from the fish with both these methods will usually be firm pulls, but they can sometimes be quite savage. It is very relaxed fishing, with each cast taking up to several minutes to be fished out and the angler gently drawing in only just enough line to ensure contact with the flies at all times. With the possibility of such firm takes it can be very exciting and rewarding.

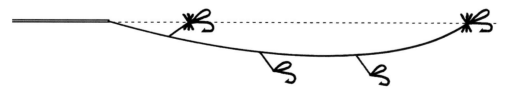

The 'washing line' method.

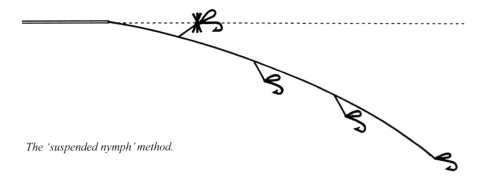

The 'suspended nymph' method.

Indications of the 'Take'

What if a trout should decide to take our fly, how do we know and what do we do? There are many different ways in which a trout reveals the fact that it has taken our artificial into its mouth, and in every case the angler should simply tighten into the fish and then keep a tight line until it is safely in the net. 'Strike' is not a word that is really applicable, as too heavy-handed an approach will only lead to either a broken leader or else the hook tearing free. A firm tightening is usually all that is needed to pull the hook home, and many times the trout will have already hooked themselves by the take or by pulling against the drag of the fly line, which due to its large diameter is quite considerable.

Although it is possible to see some takes visually, generally speaking in the Midlands' reservoirs it is usually not possible to see much of what is going on at the leader end of things (although there is an exception when a visual rise or a moving or dipping of the tip of the fly line is to be seen). There are a variety of reasons for this: the water is too choppy, it is too coloured, it is not possible to detect what is going on due to the long distances cast (at least with average eyesight), the tip of the fly line has sunk beneath the surface, the light conditions are poor, there is too much glare or shadow, or perhaps an intermediate or sinking line is in use that eliminates any visibility of the fly line whatsoever. As a result, most indications are at the angler's end of things. Even though it is true that the view is foreshortened, it is asking a bit much to be able to see every nudge, dip and movement of the tip of the fly line, which is 1mm wide and may be 25yd away.

The most common take is the pull where that is literally what happens: the trout pulls on the line and the angler tightens up in return. Perhaps the next most common is the lock up where everything momentarily goes tight and taut; again all that is needed in response is a firm tightening. Often what is seen is the line sliding out towards the fish, sometimes causing line wake as it slides across the surface if it is calm, and this again needs to be tightened into until the fish is felt on the end.

When fishing intermediate and sinking lines in choppy conditions when it is difficult to see what is going on, by watching the loop of line running from the rod tip into the water it is possible to see the loop straightening in much the same way that a leger fisherman sees his swingtip straighten out. A gentle strike until the fish is felt is all that is required.

With a deeply sunk intermediate or a sinking line the retrieve may develop into the angler suddenly feeling a fish on the end without any prior indications, the fish being hooked and played with no preliminary knocks, plucks or pulls being experienced. Keep a firm hold on such fish because even though they have hooked themselves against the drag of the fly line they may only be lightly pricked.

Sometimes the only indication is given by a leaping trout seen to be jumping out of the water to try and dislodge the hook, often several yards from where the flies were expected to be and before anything is felt. In response, line must be quickly gathered in until the fish is felt.

On occasion the only indication is the line moving at an angle or coming towards the angler beneath the surface. A gathering of line is all that is needed until contact is made and the fish will usually be 'on' due to line drag.

When dries are in use the indications can be more visible, and once the fish has been seen to turn down the line is simply tightened and the fish will hopefully hook itself. Too swift a response will only pull the fly out of the trout's still open mouth. On occasion trout will engulf a dry fly with so little disturbance that any visible indication of the take will go unnoticed and the angler will be blissfully unaware of what has happened until a pull at the hand is felt. Such an occurrence very often awakens the angler from his reverie with a jolt!

With all the takes, line should be drawn in with the left hand whilst at the same time raising the rod either sideways or upwards to set the hook. Striking sideways tends to result in a greater percentage of hooked fish, as direct contact with the fish is maintained. Raising the rod can lead to the angler momentarily losing touch, as the strike initially pulls against the drag of the fly line as it is lifted off the water, rather than set the hook. I do not think that the direction of the strike has much influence on whether the fish are hooked in the scissors or in the jaw.

Some of the indications listed seem to confirm the author's firm conviction that trout frequently mouth or explore the flies without the angler having any idea of what is going on. With slowly retrieved flies the problem is compounded, but if the angler manages to keep in touch at all times, and if the fish are confident, they will often hang on and draw line until eventually a pull is felt.

Direction of the Fish Affects the Strength of the 'Take'

Trout can intercept the flies coming from any angle, and the direction in which they are swimming in relation to the fly line will have a profound effect on the strength and the severity of the 'take' (*see* diagram below). (a) With a fish taking the fly and continuing to swim towards the angler the take may barely register unless and/or until it turns away. (b) If it is swimming at 90 degrees to the line, any take will tend

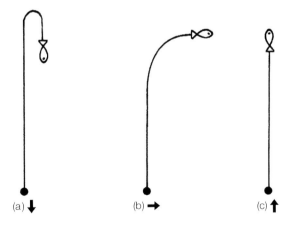

Direction of the trout and the strength of the 'take'. See text for explanation.

to register gradually as the fly line curves away; as drag builds up the water pressure prevents this curve from straightening. (c) If it is swimming away from the angler, the fish will take up any slack quite quickly and when this has all gone a firm take will result as the fish attempts to stretch the line. In this event the fish will probably hook itself. Fish swimming in this way will be responsible for most smash takes.

Fish veering off at an angle to their original course after taking will tend to be hooked in the scissors as the leader trails from the side of the mouth.

A trout that has taken confidently will often tow vast amounts of line behind it and the drag of the fly line on the fly will stop the fish from spitting the hook out if it attempts to do so. As pressure on the hook hold starts to build up the fish will feel either the hook point or the leader running alongside the side of the mouth and as a reaction it will turn away and flee. This only increases the pressure still further and may well result in the fish hooking itself.

The strength of the take often bears no relationship to the size of the fish on the end. The reason for this must be due to the fact that a small fish swimming away from the angler (c) gives a much firmer pull than a large fish that is swimming either at an angle (b) or towards the angler (a), all other things remaining equal.

Playing and Netting

What if a fish is hooked? This is the moment we have been building up to and so it is

The sight every trout angler longs to see – the rod having a nice bend as a lively fish is played out.

essential not to fail at the very last hurdle! The procedure for playing trout is much like playing any other fish except that, pound for pound, trout fight harder than most and they take to the air regularly in a way that no coarse fish ever does. The sight of a leaping trout is guaranteed to set the adrenaline going of any fly fisher, no matter how many trout they have caught in their career.

Keeping the rod at an angle to the fish to absorb any shocks and lunges is imperative, and when a leaping trout returns to the water let the rod follow it down to avoid breakage, but always keeping a bend in the rod by holding it at an angle to the line and in contact with the fish. If the trout are given any slack line they will soon and inevitably shake the hook free; if they are held too hard the hook will tear out or the leader will break. Trout have bony mouths and if the hook is not embedded in the scissors or in gristle it will only take a light hold and sometimes a fish will come unstuck for no apparent reason. Unfortunately we have no way of knowing what sort of hook hold there is until the fish is finally in the net.

Trout should be played firmly, but always be ready to give line and let the fish go if it wants to until it is finally played out. Trying to hold a fish that wants to run is a major cause of them getting free. The fish should not be brought in too close, too quickly, but rather be allowed to tire itself out away from the angler, and kept well away from the drogue or anchor rope if boat fishing.

The final netting after an exciting and dogged fight. A large net makes the job so much easier and safer.

Safely in the net at last!

When it eventually does see you it may well try and bolt, but if it is tired when this happens it is less likely to have the energy to escape. Keep as low as possible and try not to present a high profile, which will only alarm the fish.

Netting should be done smoothly and confidently, letting the trout know who is boss. Keep its head up and slide it positively over the submerged net ring, but always be ready for any final and sudden attempt to escape. Once the fish is safely over the rim the net should be raised and the fish will drop safely into the meshes.

Once it is safely on the bank, you can breathe a sigh of relief and despatch the fish by administering two or three firm blows to the head before admiring it. After all the time and effort it took to catch, you have deserved that fish, so bask a moment or two in your own personal glory.

Two Fish Hooked at the Same Time

Sooner or later two trout will be hooked at the same time. Providing they are not too large it can be great fun because you are never 100 per cent in charge. Keep in contact and let the fish tire themselves out against each other.

When it is time for netting, try to net the top dropper fish first, and then draw the

Catching larger trout is a bit like waiting for a bus – a long wait and then two at a time!
This superb trout was caught 90min before the 7½lb fish shown on the frontispiece.

A limit from Eyebrook Reservoir. We should not expect a limit every time, but they are nevertheless welcome when they do come.

net towards you and smartly snip the nylon close to the fly; then you will be in contact with the second fish, which can now be played and netted. With a bit of good fortune it is often possible to net both fish, but if one or maybe both of them escape it has to be accepted philosophically. Some things happen when we are fly fishing that are out of our control, and our sport is all the richer for it.

A Quick Limit Bag!

On those occasions when we have managed to get a few fish quickly, probably the best thing to do is to use the time to do a bit of experimenting with flies, techniques and parts of the reservoir that have not given us success before, and so bolster our confidence for the future. Merely banging out eight fish in quick succession using exactly the same flies and method will not teach us very much.

Although we should not expect a limit bag every time, when we do get one they do bolster our confidence (that is until the next time when we are struggling for a pull) and if we really want one, we should complete it while we can.

I well remember one of my first limits at Eyebrook in the days before catch and release, when I had to stop fishing at number seven well before half past ten and go back to the lodge to pass the time with Andy Miller. I was expecting my wife to arrive at lunchtime with a picnic, and she was looking forward to going out in the afternoon in the boat; although she does not fish she nevertheless enjoys going out when the weather is fine. After a long and relaxing lunch at the lodge we finally went out, I speedily to complete my limit and my wife to catch a bit of the sun – and you can guess the rest. It took two hours to get that final fish!

Blanks

Blanks are a fact of fly fishing life and we all get one from time to time no matter how experienced we are, and rather than being frustrated we should try and look at them from a positive angle and learn from our mistakes. Those successful angling journalists, who to read their columns in the angling magazines seem to get a limit bag every time, may not always be 100 per cent

The new lodge at Thornton Reservoir with its distinctive roof in the form of an upturned boat.

truthful. Isn't it strange that when they turn up at our local water they don't seem to fare any better than the rest of us?

All the same, there is nothing more disheartening than to come back to the lodge to record a nil return, especially when those who have booked out before you have had a hatful. We know that at those times when we get a limit it is as a result of our clinical reasoning, our focused dedication and our superior fishing skills; whereas when it's the other fellow who has a bagful, and we couldn't get a pull, it was simply because he happened to be over a shoal of suicidal fish who would take anything thrown at them! Try and congratulate those lucky fellows with a bit of grace – and without treading on their rods or tripping them up on the boat dock and holding them under.

A bit of humility never does us any harm, and when you think you have finally cracked it, the trout will always bring you down to earth with a bump. Long may they do so.

Line Bites and Foul-Hooked Fish

There is a take that is not a true take at all; it is caused by fish swimming and bumping into the line and giving a false indication. When this occurs the fish may be felt, but however much line is drawn in the point is never reached when the fish is 'on'. The coarse angler would refer to these as 'line bites'. When this phenomenon occurs, examine the hooks carefully. A fish scale or fish slime on the point will often confirm that this is what has happened.

To give a typical example of this sort of occurrence: at the start of the season when fish are congregating in large numbers in very shallow water, the fly line can be laid over the backs of large numbers of fish that are not actually feeding and, although indications are frequent, takes are few. No true sportsman deliberately wants to damage or foul-hook a fish, and if it becomes a serious problem then a change in tactics, perhaps to smaller flies, to a slower retrieve, or even moving fishing position to a different spot, may be necessary.

On occasion a fish will be foul-hooked, and because the trout cannot be turned as a fish hooked in the mouth can they consequently make frequent dashes towards the horizon. Such fish always give the impression that they are much larger than they really are. Many a trout that has fought like a monster and has brought visions of a glass-case specimen whilst being played has eventually turned out to be merely a foul-hooked fish!

8 On the Bank: An Enquiring Mind and Some Important Questions

In the discussions on tackle in previous chapters we omitted to mention perhaps the most important piece of equipment that any angler can possess – an enquiring and analytical mind. It is all too easy to have a few tried and tested tactics that work some of the time, but if we stick to them when the conditions are not appropriate we will never succeed consistently. However, once 'chuck and chance' methods are left behind, the way is opened up to an array of different approaches that will make fishing more thought provoking, more varied, more interesting and ultimately far more successful.

It may be stating the obvious, but no matter how good our casting is, how good the artificial fly is, and how well it is presented, if there are no trout in the vicinity of our fly then we are simply wasting our time. We can pick a spot and fish away monotonously, as many do hour after hour, in the vain hope that a trout will eventually swim by and take our offering. It may well do so in the end, but that is not a good use of time and effort and will only lead to limited success. It is neither a productive nor a satisfying way to fish.

Successful fishing is all about spending the time in the most profitable manner possible. In order that the time is used productively, there are some basic, but very vital, questions that need to be asked whenever we go fishing. These are:

1   Which location shall we fish?
2   Where in the reservoir are the fish?
3   At what depth are the fish?
4   Are they feeding and, if they are, on what?
5   If they are not feeding, what is needed to provoke a reaction so that they will take our offerings?

To fish successfully, it is vital to answer these simple questions correctly. So let us ask each one in turn.

1   Which Location shall We Fish?

Nowadays most parts of the country are blessed with a number of reservoirs and lakes open to the day-ticket trout angler, and if a range of venues is available the choice of where to fish should be made wisely. Time should be taken to get to know the fishery staff, who will be pleased to give information about catches, stocking rates and fishery policy, as well as successful methods, flies and productive areas.

To get to know any water and its foibles well, it has to be fished on a regular basis, in both good and bad conditions, throughout the whole season. This could lead, if

Andy Miller, the fishery manager at Eyebrook Reservoir and a first-rate angler, with a sleek 9lb 12oz rainbow.

caution is not taken, to becoming a 'one-water' man; one who is at ease at his 'home' fishery but who is all at sea when faced with another water and a totally different set of conditions. To be versatile it is necessary, on the one hand, to have some variety in one's fishing, but, on the other, not to make the grave error of chasing the returns and hopping from water to water in the hope of always fishing the one that is currently producing the big catches. Being a member of a local fishing club, where valuable contacts can be made, can be a great help. Its members will be fishing a wide variety of fisheries, and suggestions of where to fish and how to go about it will generally be forthcoming.

In addition to day-ticket fisheries there are also a few large waters that are run by private syndicates and fishing clubs, and membership does become available from time to time. They are generally more expensive to join, and the advantages and disadvantages need to be considered carefully before applying.

2 Where in the Reservoir are the Fish?

Trout are never evenly spread out over a body of water such as a reservoir; to the contrary, some areas will hold the vast bulk of the fish, sometimes very tightly shoaled,

'The Bell' at Eyebrook Reservoir – one of the 'hotspots' at this famous fishery.

whereas other parts will hold very few or none at all. To confirm this you only need to go over a body of water with a fishfinder to see that in some places they show up in huge numbers, whereas other areas are barren and fishless. There are many pointers to help get the answer to fish location right. Each one will be looked at in turn.

Firstly, fish might be rising and so it is possible to know instantly where they are. Fish that are not actually rising but are cruising near the surface can also reveal themselves by an unnatural movement, or indeed a flattening, of the water as they turn beneath it. The angler should look and observe.

The presence of birds such as swallows, swifts and martins will often indicate where insects are hatching, and gulls will congregate where shoals of fry are located. If in doubt, fish where the birds are.

Keeping an eye open to what is happening to other anglers on the water is also worthwhile, and the sight of others catching fish is a positive indication of where the trout might be. We should not, as a matter of courtesy, breathe down their necks, but we can discreetly station ourselves in the general vicinity, provided that we do not disturb either them or their fish.

There are also seasonal patterns that tell us where the trout are likely to be. This is dealt with in greater detail in Chapter 15, but in general terms the trout tend to be in the margins during the early part of the season until early summer when they will start to migrate to the offshore body of the lake, although not necessarily into deeper

We should all try and help our fellow anglers whenever we can. The late Dave Hughes of Rothwell – always a source of advice and encouragement.

water. They return to the margins once again towards the end of the season when the fry start to congregate there. This is why bank fishing can be so profitable in early season, dropping off in high summer, only to become profitable again in late August, September and October.

These are only generalizations, however, because the seasonal cycles of weather conditions do fluctuate, and their corresponding influence on the fish can be changed by any unusual weather pattern, which can either bring forward or delay the normal cycle.

Most lakes and reservoirs have what anglers term 'hot spots', where the fish are known to congregate regularly, and knowledge of where these places are is crucial information. At any reputable fishery the staff will know these places and will pass this knowledge on to visitors, as it is in their own interests for customers to catch fish and as a result come back again. The same hot spots may not necessarily be productive throughout the whole season, and such things as temperature, wind direction, seasonal migrations, and even recent stockings can often upset the best of predictions. A polite request for information will usually be greeted with helpful suggestions of where to fish, what methods to try and which flies to employ.

Looking into the fishery returns sheet for the previous day will often show what methods and flies have been working and may be worth a try, although the same pattern will not necessarily follow 2 days running. If you do manage to have a profitable day, jot any helpful information down so that other anglers can benefit from your experience. I do not subscribe to the notion that everything should be kept secret; we are all brother and sister anglers and should try to help one another whenever possible.

Features and structure

Trout like to hold up in places where there are weed beds, bottom irregularities or something similar. Such places possibly give them some reference point, but more probably give them a feeling of extra security from predators. This can be confirmed when a fishfinder is drifted over an apparently featureless expanse of water. When some kind of irregularity on the bottom is located, there will usually be a fish or two lying close to it. This tells us that we should endeavour to locate any bottom features if we are to find the fish, and it goes some way to explain why one area is full of fish and another close by and seemingly similar is devoid of them.

Features on the bank are often carried out into the water, and this is where, unless we have better and more reliable local information, we should make a start. Things to look out for on the bank include:

- Promontories stretching out into the water.
- Lines of hedges or trees.

- Ridges or raised contours.
- Steep banks dropping into deep water.
- Depressions or lowered contours.
- Old roads, paths or tracks.
- Streams and ditches.

Things to look out for on the water include:

- Weed beds.
- Islands and offshore shoals.
- Draw-off towers and aerators.
- Fish cages.

We are looking for something that is a little out of the ordinary and therefore might be a holding point for the trout.

In drought conditions, when water levels are low, it is a good idea to walk round the places that are regularly fished, noting features that are now visible but in normal conditions will be below the water line. They may be worth a try when water levels return to normal.

Water surface irregularities

Can the water itself tell us anything that will help us know where to start? Looked at with an observant eye, a reservoir is never a mere featureless expanse; there are always differences and nuances in the surface ripple that can tell a great deal. It is wise to spend a few moments before fishing to look across the water, segment by segment, to see what can be learnt.

Such things as calm lanes among the ripples are areas where localized hatches can occur, and they have long been recognized as places where surface-feeding trout may well be seeking emerging insects. Exactly what causes calm lanes is open to debate. They probably do not always occur as a result of the wind funnelling around trees and contours in the vicinity – the author has observed them on a calm day in mid

Fish cages at Rutland Water.

Atlantic, over 1,000 miles from the nearest land! For tackle concealment it is a wise precaution to cast towards the near side of the unruffled portion so that the fly line is lying in the rippled water where it will be less visible, rather than laying it across the calm water where it can show up like an anchor rope.

Similarly, scum lanes, revealed by lines of bubbles that stretch out down the path of the wind, sometimes for great distances, can be inhabited by fish as they seek out food trapped in the thicker and less penetrable surface film. Drifting down such lanes can be very productive.

Even when there is a breeze, there can be large patches of sheltered water where the surface is calm and still. Fishing in such water can be difficult; firstly, the fish tend to avoid such areas because they are more visible to predators, and, secondly, when they are present they can spot the angler more easily and as a consequence will take evasive action. The better option is often to head for the ripple, where the breaking up of the outlines by the waves helps concealment.

Upwind or downwind shore?

Trout (and hatching insects) prefer to be where the water temperature is to their liking, and the action of the wind determines where this preferred water is likely to be. Warm water rises to the surface (as it is less dense) and cooler water sinks. As

82

Calm lane amid the ripple.

Scum lane in coloured water off the Hambleton Peninsular at Rutland Water.

water is a poor conductor, and does not mix easily, different layers can be at widely different temperatures. The diagram below illustrates the phenomenon.

When there is warm sunshine and the air is still, the surface layer of water will warm up but the lower levels will remain cold. Due to the lack of wind the two layers will remain separate (a). The surface temperature of the water around the reservoir will be similar and fishing either bank could be equally profitable.

When there is a breeze, the surface layer of warmed water will be blown to the downwind shore and cold water from the deeps will replace it on the upwind side (b). It is not uncommon for the water to be warm on one side of the reservoir and quite cold on the other. Most reservoirs are irregular in shape and depth and predicting where the warm water will be is not always as easy as it sounds. To compound matters further the wind continually changes force and direction, and the contours of the reservoir

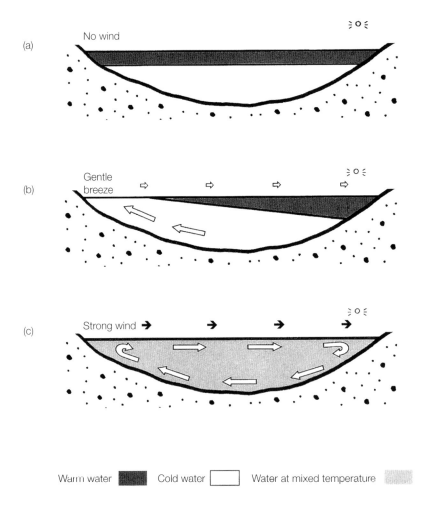

Distribution of water at various wind strengths. (a) Calm conditions. (b) Gentle breeze. (c) Strong wind.

bed can channel the flow unpredictably. Often the only reliable way is to physically test the water to see how warm it is. On those occasions when the wind is strong over a period of time, the water will tend to mix and it will be at a more constant temperature throughout (c).

When the air and the wind are cold, the surface water will be cooled and then sink. This water will be replaced by warmer water, which again is cooled and in turn sinks; the process is repeated as the water temperature gradually falls.

Choosing which bank to fish is important, and at different times the upwind or downwind shore will prove to be the most productive depending on the temperature the trout are looking for. Casting into the wind is not as easy as when the wind is coming from behind, but if that is where the fish are, that is the place to be.

3 At what Depth are the Fish?

Once we have made a decision and arrived at an area on the reservoir where the fish are likely to be, we then have to decide at what depth the fish will probably be located.

When trout are feeding they can be taking food on the bottom, in mid water, just subsurface, actually in the surface film, or alternatively taking food forms resting on the surface. They have also been known to take such things as adult damsels while they are flying or hovering above the water, but as a fishing tactic that can be dismissed as impractical. Unless the trout are showing themselves at the surface, it will be necessary to use a little logical deduction to determine where they might be by deciding where their food will probably be located, where their preferred water temperature is, and where the level of light will be to their liking. A systematic searching of all the depths will eventually find the fish, but if the angler has a good idea of where to

concentrate his efforts it will probably save a good deal of time.

As a rule, trout tend to cruise at fixed depths, sometimes covering relatively large areas in the process, and they move around in this horizontal plane rather than moving up and down in a vertical one. In view of this it is important to fish the layer that the fish are occupying and not above or below it. Coarse anglers know only too well the difference that moving a float up or down a few inches (and sometimes even a fraction of an inch) can make. It is therefore crucial to ensure that our fly is at the same depth as the trout. The eyes of trout are situated so that they tend to look straight ahead and above, and if we are unsure at what depth they are it is better to fish the flies a little too shallow, rather than too deep, as they will be silhouetted against the surface and therefore more visible.

4 Are the Trout Feeding and, if They are, on What?

Trout are opportunist feeders and are to be found feeding anywhere from shallow water (and sometimes exceedingly shallow water of just a few inches) through to the very deepest water at various times of the day or the year depending on the prevailing seasonal, weather and water conditions. They will feed on virtually anything that is edible providing they can ingest it, whether it be an insect, crustacean, water bug, fish fry or water weed, as well as stones, feathers, leaves, twigs, pieces of wood, plastic, even cigarette ends (one way of having instant smoked trout perhaps!) and other inedible items that the author has personally witnessed in the stomach of trout over the years. It would make interesting reading to collate all the hundreds of nonedible items that have been found inside trout. Although it might be fascinating,

Even moderately sized trout have large mouths, and they can engulf pretty well anything a fly angler can throw at them. The fly shown here was tied on a size 4 longshank hook.

it probably wouldn't help us improve our catch rates in any way.

In spite of their catholic feeding habits, however, they will not be feeding everywhere, and on everything, all at the same time. That is why the location of feeding fish, and an inspired guess as to what they are taking, is an essential skill in any successful angler's portfolio. Nevertheless, just a few food forms make up the vast bulk of the items that trout regularly feed on, plus a few seasonal ones, and these will be looked at in depth in Chapter 10.

Rise forms

Trout that are seen to be visibly rising or disturbing the water can give further clues. The surface of a reservoir is an area with defined zones, and different insects will be located in different parts. The trout will be seen to rise in visibly different ways depending on what their food is and where it is located.

Not all rise forms are the same and understanding the differences (and why they are different) gives indications of where the trout's food is and the creatures they are pursuing. The fact that trout are seen to be rising does not necessarily mean that they are taking adult flies on the surface; indeed it is more likely that they will be taking hatching nymphs and pupae *in* the surface film.

Generally, the slower and smoother the rise form, the smaller and more immobile the creature and the lower it will be located in relation to the surface film (e.g. emerging buzzer pupae, shucks, spent flies and terrestrials trapped in the film). On the other hand, the more violent and splashy rises tend to be as a result of larger and/or more active creatures on the surface (e.g. sedges and daddies).

Narrowing down the alternatives

From the list of possibilities we need to narrow down the alternatives by deciding what is likely to be present, identifying what is in, on and around the water, ascertaining what any fish caught have been feeding on, drawing from previous experience (this is where keeping fishing records can be helpful) and doing a little logical thinking. Arriving at the correct conclusion as to what the trout are targeting at any particular moment may take a little time and effort, but it is not beyond the capability of most of us. Getting this right not only leads to larger catches, it also brings greater satisfaction.

5 If the Trout are not Feeding, what is Needed to Provoke a Reaction so They will Take Our Offerings?

There are times when the trout do not appear to feed at all. This may be because they are digesting what they have already taken, the water temperature is too high for them and they have become lethargic, the water temperature has dropped, perhaps due to a very heavy fall of cold rainwater, or simply because they have chosen not to feed. Nevertheless, in spite of the fact that they are not feeding it does not mean that they are uncatchable; it may not be easy – but they can still be caught.

Trout are extremely curious fish, and we can exploit their curiosity with appropriate lures should it become necessary. Curiosity must be the reason and the explanation why trout will swallow some of the most garish of lures, which they surely cannot be taking because they think they are a natural food form. This approach has already been discussed in Chapter 6.

This in-built curiosity must surely be the reason why we are able to catch, on a fly or a spinner, their close relatives, the migratory Atlantic salmon, which never feed in fresh water once they have returned to the rivers to spawn (indeed they are physically incapable of feeding as their stomachs atrophy at this time). Some say that the tendency to take lures is a demonstration of aggression rather than mere curiosity, but I believe in the curiosity theory as the most appropriate explanation for this singular, but otherwise inexplicable behaviour.

Conclusions

The above five questions may appear to be straightforward; and sometimes they are relatively easy to answer. On other occasions they can be difficult, and it will take much thought and experimenting before we arrive at the correct conclusions. Nevertheless, getting the answers right does hold the key to improved reservoir catches.

9 Valuable Information Straight from the Fish's Mouth

Trout are opportunist feeders with a varied diet, and spooning the fish and performing an autopsy gives the angler important clues to their feeding habits. What is in their stomach is what they have been eating prior to being caught: it is as plain and as straightforward as that. It is *fact* and not conjecture, and so it is appropriate that this simple but vital task is looked at further.

The use of the marrow spoon has been advocated in fly fishing literature over many years, and so it is surprising that its use is still rarely witnessed on the banks today. Why this should be is a bit of a mystery, because it can give the angler who troubles to use one valuable information, which is literally 'straight from the fish's mouth'. It is interesting to note that often when the author has performed an autopsy on the bank many anglers have come over to witness it and comment on what is found, in spite of the fact that, in the main, they do not appear to perform autopsies themselves.

The whole ethic of fly fishing is based on the premise of offering the trout something that it will take into its mouth, so that it can be hooked and landed. Knowing what the fish are feeding on at any particular time must surely be of great value.

The Diet of Trout

We do know that trout are extremely catholic in their diet and that they regularly feed on such diverse items as nymphs, larvae, snails, fish fry, daphnia, beetles, crustaceans, winged flies, terrestrials and so on. They are carnivorous creatures in their normal feeding patterns most of the time, although they will take vegetable matter as well. This is in addition to some of the more gaudy and garish lures that resemble nothing that God ever created on this earth, but which are successfully employed to catch them from time to time. Nevertheless, in spite of this unpredictable but not uncharacteristic behaviour, knowing what the trout are feeding on, and then employing a fly that effectively suggests, caricatures or mimics it, gives the angler a basis from which to start.

Those anglers who have no definite idea of what the trout are taking, and who have nothing but memory or vague guesswork on which to base their hypotheses, must surely be at a disadvantage. This is especially true on those occasions when the fish are feeding selectively; not that this occurs as often as we might suppose, but it does happen.

The Marrow Spoon

Fly fishermen are fortunate to have the marrow spoon – a simple but invaluable tool. It will reveal at a glance exactly what the fish are feeding on and gives this important information in an instant. In this respect the fly angler is at a distinct advantage over the coarse angler, who catches and releases his fish and is therefore unable to perform autopsies. This does presuppose that the angler catches at least one fish to study at the outset, but that is another matter altogether!

Conducting an autopsy on a fish is such a simple and clean procedure (certainly far less messy than gutting a fish) that it is surprising that there are still anglers around who do not even carry a marrow spoon, let alone use one. The word autopsy is perhaps an unfortunate choice of word, conjuring up gruesome associations of bodies and mortuaries, which in truth does not match up to the reality of the procedure.

Choice of marrow spoon

The marrow spoon (or marrow scoop) is a simple and cheap affair and numerous designs, usually made from metal or plastic, are available from virtually every fly fishing shop nowadays. At one time they were difficult items to procure but fortunately that is no longer the case.

Some are simply spoons whereas others are incorporated into a combination priest. It does not matter which type is chosen so long as the bowl is deep enough, it is shaped in such a way that the contents can be collected and withdrawn easily, and the handle is long enough to cope with a large fish; with a short handle it can be difficult to insert the spoon deep enough to reach fully into the fish's stomach. A 10¼in marrow spoon (which is longer than most available) was only just long enough to reach into the stomach of a 23in trout and extract the contents. The fish weighed almost 5lb.

The author suggests that two cheap marrow spoons are better than one expensive one as they do tend to get mislaid.

Method of spooning

The procedure for obtaining a spooning for examination is quite straightforward. After the fish has been caught and despatched – autopsies should never be carried out on live fish and so their use is not applicable to catch and release methods – the marrow spoon is carefully inserted into the trout's mouth and pushed gently about 6in down the gullet until a slight resistance is felt. With a little practice this place can be found easily. The spoon is then rotated two or three times and brought into a position with the bowl facing upwards – it can be useful to mark this position on the handle if it cannot otherwise be easily identified – and the spoon and its contents are carefully withdrawn. The remains of the trout's last meal will be plain to see.

On many occasions the spoon will be completely full of matter, and so a repetition of the procedure will be necessary to get a full picture of the trout's feeding pattern. It is generally assumed that the items that are nearer the shoulder of the spoon have been eaten more recently than those near the tip, and that being so it is even possible to judge how the fish's feeding pattern has altered during the course of the day.

The entire operation takes only a few moments and is virtually mess free; no blood should be encountered if it is done correctly.

Interpreting the results

The contents of the spoon can be examined whilst they are still in the spoon, tapped out onto the hand, or for detailed examination emptied into a small, shallow, white

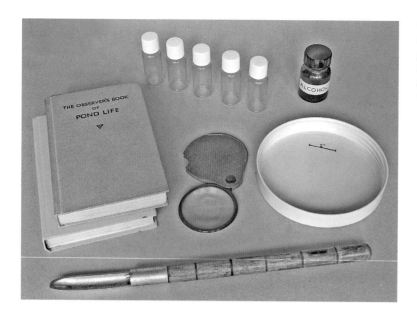

Carrying a marrow spoon is essential. A magnifying glass, field guide and a few sample tubes take up little space in the tackle bag but can prove invaluable.

or clear dish containing a small amount of water. The mass will separate quite easily in the water, which considerably facilitates identification.

With a little experience it is easy to identify most of the items at a glance, although in the early learning stages a small pocket magnifying glass can be helpful. It can also be useful if one comes across unfamiliar items at any time which one wishes to identify positively in conjunction with a field guide.

Spooning will often yield a number of live specimens – buzzer pupae and corixae being common examples – among the rest of the trout's diet. Observing the manner of movement of these is useful so that we can better try and imitate, with our artificials, what is observed. How so many of these fragile creatures manage to survive in the stomach of the fish is a matter of conjecture, but they regularly do.

There will be times when the food will largely have been digested, and what remains is a mass of slime, but with a little careful observation (perhaps with the aid of the magnifying glass) it is possible to pick out features of recognition among the undigested fragments. Under such circumstances it is as well to remind ourselves that when the trout start feeding again it may well be to a different feeding pattern.

On occasion a lot of bottom debris will be found in the autopsies along with the food items, and this tells us where the fish have been feeding and consequently where we should be fishing our flies.

If required, samples can be transferred into specimen tubes containing a preservative (clear alcohol such as diluted white rum perhaps being the most convenient) and be taken home for further study or referred to at the fly-tying bench. It should be remembered, however, that the use of preservative (and keeping samples in the light) tends to destroy the coloration over a period of time and this fact needs to be borne in mind when matching colours.

Illustrations of Autopsies

The photographs of the autopsies on the following pages are reproduced to show typical examples of the sort of thing to be expected in the stomach of an average trout.

This autopsy from a boat-caught rainbow trout in April showed that it had been feeding exclusively on daphnia. With over 900 separate but identical food items present, it could rightly be described as an example of selective feeding.

The stomach contents of a bank-caught rainbow in May, which had been feeding on black buzzer pupae, caddis larvae, freshwater louse, a few bloodworm, a damsel larva and a buzzer shuck.

An assortment of aquatic life, including damsel larvae, freshwater louse, bloodworm, buzzer pupae, a leech and a caddis larva, were all found inside one bank-caught rainbow trout.

Buzzer pupae will be present in a large proportion of autopsies. Some of the pupae here are on the point of hatching, and the red haemoglobin 'blow' of the wing buds is faintly visible.

This 1lb 9oz rainbow had swallowed a perch that was almost 4in long. Boat fishing at Thornton Reservoir in mid September.

After 2 days of continuous rain and an extra foot of water in the margins, this bank-caught fish had been feeding mainly on earthworms. It was taken on a Black & Green Holographic Buzzer.

Bloodworm predominated in this spooning of a booby-caught rainbow taken on the bottom in 24ft of water. It also contained a few buzzer pupae and a lot of bottom debris. Boat fishing on a cold day in May with a north wind.

Trout are not carnivorous all the time. This October autopsy from a trout caught on a Black & Green Holographic Buzzer contained four separate pieces of weed, one beetle, one tiny shuck and one buzzer pupa.

This spooning from a trout caught on the bottom in 26ft of water was full of buzzer pupae. Curiously, it had a live corixa in its stomach (circled), which was swimming around quite happily. Corixae are only to be found in water less than 3ft deep.

An autopsy from a rainbow that had been feeding mainly on terrestrial beetles and bugs. Although it appears to have been feeding somewhat selectively, the contents range in size from tiny to large.

This rainbow contained just one revolting-looking horse leech (haemopsis) that was 3¾in long. It was taken on a deeply fished Black & Green Fritz Tadpole while boat fishing in July.

Literally dozens of tiny olive buzzer pupae and bloodworm were present in this spooning taken from a rainbow caught on a Rough GRHE. Boat fishing in early June.

The autopsy from a rainbow from Ringstead Grange. It was stuffed to the gills with damsel larvae and a few bloodworm. Boat fishing in June.

As the results of this September autopsy of a 1lb 12oz boat-caught rainbow taken off the 'island' at Eyebrook Reservoir show, trout really do take feathers as part of their diet! It should give us confidence to believe that our concoctions of fur and feather do work.

As can be seen, the amount of detail and information that can be gleaned is significant, and the lack of mess is plainly obvious.

With such a wealth of helpful evidence that can be gathered quickly and easily, it is unwise to ignore this enlightening procedure. It is hoped the illustrations will spur the reader to purchase and use a marrow spoon on a regular basis. The dish shown in the photographs has a diameter of 4½in.

Autopsies of trout caught from the bank tend to reveal a wider variety of food items than those of fish caught from the boats. The reason for this is that the margins are by far the most productive part of any stillwater and will be host to practically every food item that the trout are likely to consume. Once deeper water is encountered, those creatures that are unable to survive at any depth will be absent. Because shallow water is much more productive, commercial fish farmers invariably use shallow rearing ponds, rather than deep ones, to obtain the optimum yield per acre.

Fish that are Empty

On occasion a trout will be completely empty, and on analysing my records I was surprised to find that this occurs more frequently than I had previously supposed. On one occasion, five out of six fish that were retained from Ringstead Grange Trout Fishery in June were empty. There are at least four (and probably many more) reasons for this phenomenon.

Firstly, fish that have only recently been stocked may not yet have learned how to hunt and forage in the wild (especially if they have come straight from the hatchery rather than from fish cages or stock ponds on site). Until this skill has been learned they will be empty. Trout pellets appear to be digested quickly by the fish, and they have a high nutritional and carbohydrate content that enables the trout to store sufficient quantities of energy in their bodies for their immediate needs. Until this energy has been expended there will be no need to replace it. Trout are carnivores, which, unlike herbivores, tend to eat in spasmodic bursts rather than graze continually.

Secondly, trout are cold-blooded creatures and have a body temperature that is determined by that of the surrounding water. When temperatures are very low they will be torpid and consequently unwilling to feed. During such a state they will move around very little, expend little energy and, consequently, will have no need to feed, with the result that their stomachs will be empty. We may catch such fish occasionally, but this will probably be by appealing to their curiosity rather than their feeding instinct.

Thirdly, when the water is very warm (anything above 20°C: *see* Chapter 15, p.165) the fish seem to go off the feed. It follows that after they have digested any food that is already present in their stomachs they will remain empty until the conditions change and they start to feed once more.

Fourthly, there are times when trout do not feed for any obvious reason. Although we cannot explain why this happens, large numbers of trout do fast quite regularly, and as a consequence their stomachs will be empty.

Conclusions

Once we know what the trout are feeding on, we can decide what flies to employ and whether a change in tactics is necessary. There is always the dilemma of 'do we change a winning team or not?' when we discover that the fish have been taking something completely different to our successful fly! This is one of those brain-teasing dilemmas of fly fishing, but it is one that makes it so interesting. With a three-fly leader one is able to hedge one's bets to some extent, and this can help in predicaments such as this and offers a compromise solution.

With experience, the results of the spoonings will often be what we would expect to see, but there are also times when the results are surprising. For example, on one occasion several fish contained nothing but daphnia, until one seemingly identical fish, caught in exactly the same area and in the same way, contained no daphnia at all but only flying ants. Was this a different strain of fish with different feeding habits? Or perhaps it had found an ant hatch and fed on it until it ended and then rejoined the other fish? Was it more inclined to surface feeding? Or was there some other explanation? This occurrence could possibly be an example of a preoccupied feeding pattern by this individual fish, but it was not caught on an ant pattern but a size 14 Silver Corixa!

It is observations such as these that make us realize that we are often scratching the surface of angling knowledge and will (fortunately for the sport) never have all the answers; our speculations are sometimes merely interesting conjecture. The positive aspect is that they do get us thinking for ourselves rather than blindly following other anglers' formulae (which are just as likely to prove as incorrect as ours). This helps us in our endeavours to try and think like the trout and so catch more of them.

After all the trouble taken to deceive our first fish and discover what it has been taking, it is necessary to sound a note of caution against making any hasty changes.

It is probably best to continue with the successful set-up for a quarter of an hour or so and see what happens. If no further takes are forthcoming, that is the time to consider whether any changes are necessary. Different flies behave differently in the water depending on their size, shape and weight, and a change of fly could possibly alter the profile the leader takes in a way that makes the presentation less attractive rather than the reverse.

The Accumulation of Knowledge

Part of the delight of fly fishing, one that makes it the great sport that it is, is the gradual accumulation of experience, skill and knowledge over the years. The use of autopsies in our attempts to try and deceive the trout are invaluable in helping us to achieve that aim. The regular practice of performing autopsies should therefore be an integral part of any regular fish-catching routine.

There is no doubt that to be able to identify the fish's diet, to tie on an artificial fly that caricatures or matches the real thing, and then catch a fish on it as a result, is a cause for great personal satisfaction. It is the epitome of the whole ethos of what fly fishing is all about, rather than the mere accumulation of large bags.

I suggest that if any readers have not yet started to perform autopsies, they do try and make a start at the earliest opportunity. The results, both in the number of trout caught and in the extra enjoyment obtained, will be more than worth the effort involved.

10 The Food of Reservoir Trout: Quantity and Frequency

It is now appropriate to look at the various food items that trout feed on and see what that means in terms of fishing tactics.

This is a book on fly fishing, not a book on entomology, and therefore what follows will be solely on a level of practical fishing application rather than pure scientific knowledge. The reader may wish to delve into the scientific aspects of water life in more detail, and it is a fascinating subject, but for practical angling purposes this is not necessary and so will not be dealt with here.

The whole premise of looking at things from the aspect of what the trout wants, and not what the angler would like to give it, will of necessity affect everything that will be considered. As a result, the food items that will be discussed in this chapter will be restricted to a reasonably compact minimum, but this will be all that will be needed. We shall be referring to a table d'hôte menu, rather than a full à la carte one, and this chapter will, as a consequence, be both practical and mercifully short!

Quantity and Frequency

The relative importance of each individual food item will be assessed, based on the quantity and frequency in which they occur inside the trout. This may result in some of the various food items being relegated to secondary tactics, or perhaps ignored altogether, but this is necessary if we wish to follow the principle of giving the trout something similar to that on which they are known to be feeding.

The data that follow stem from the results of thousands of spoonings that have been personally carried out by the author, on innumerable trout, over a number of years.

Some of the emergence dates given and summarized in the tables at the end of the chapter may differ from what has been published in the past, but they are offered as a result of practical first-hand observations and not by copying existing information that may not be appropriate as it may refer to other locations. These data apply to the Midlands' reservoirs and lakes, and waters of a similar nature in other parts of the country. For other locations a different set of parameters will apply and they should be adjusted in the light of local experience.

Identification

The drawings in this chapter will help the angler to correctly identify the results of his autopsies. The distinguishing points of identification for each particular creature are such that they should speak for

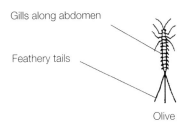

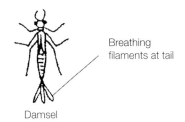

Gills along abdomen

Feathery tails

Olive

Breathing filaments at tail

Damsel

Features distinguishing olive nymph and damsel larva.

themselves. They are all quite unique and different from each other, and in most cases once they have been seen and identified in the flesh as it were, they will be easily recognized again.

The only situation where there could possibly be any doubt would be in the case of damsel larvae and olive nymphs, which could possibly be confused. There is, however, a distinct difference in their tails. Olives have true, feathery tails whereas damsels have much thicker and stubbier breathing filaments at the tail region. In addition, olives possess gills running along the sides of the abdomen whereas damsels do not. Damsels are much sturdier creatures in comparison to the more delicately proportioned olives; although as such comparisons are subjective, they are not as reliable as physical features, which cannot be mistaken.

The drawings shown here are roughly life size, except for daphnia, which is far too small to pick out any features of reference with the naked eye, although once seen it is easily recognized again. These are merely 'generic' representations of the groups of creatures, and are shown for recognition purposes. Within each particular group there are, in most cases, a multitude of individual species. Identification of these species is the realm of the scientist and entomologist; for practical angling purposes it is unnecessary.

We will look at the major items first, followed by the lesser and short seasonal ones.

Primary Food Items

Buzzers (or midges)

On most of the lowland reservoirs, the chief food form to interest the trout is the buzzer as it is called by anglers, or chironomid to give its scientific name. This small two-winged fly forms the staple diet of the trout in its various stages, but it is the pupa that is undoubtedly the most important. It is quite common for autopsies to show

An adult buzzer. When winged buzzers are in evidence it is pretty certain that pupae will be hatching and that the trout will be feeding on them.

101

buzzer pupae inside the fish at any time of the year.

Fishing for trout that are feeding on buzzer pupae should always form a major line of attack, and the artificials to mimic them should be fished in the surface film, just below it, in mid water, or on the bottom, as the location of the naturals and hence the trout dictates. The classic static retrieve with a team of buzzer pupae has been described in Chapter 7 and is probably one of the most exciting forms of fishing for the nymph angler.

The larval stage, the bloodworm, is again on the menu throughout the whole year and, as autopsies confirm, artificials to represent them deserve to be on the leader regularly. It is strange that they are often ignored by fly fishermen despite their great popularity with the trout. If you have any doubt about the importance of the blood-worm to freshwater fish, ask a coarse fish-erman what he thinks about them!

The hatching stage, when the flies finally leave their pupal case as adults, has been the starting point for many of the recent

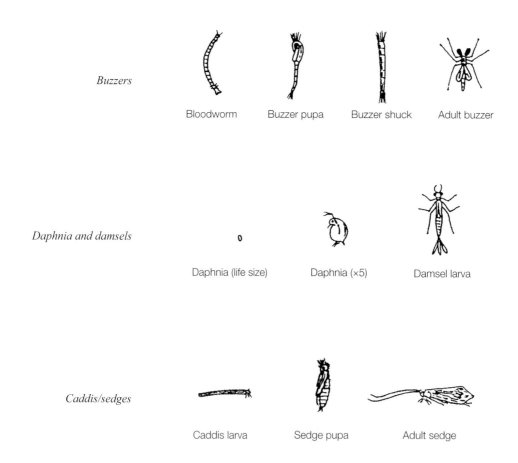

Buzzers

Bloodworm   Buzzer pupa   Buzzer shuck   Adult buzzer

Daphnia and damsels

Daphnia (life size)   Daphnia (×5)   Damsel larva

Caddis/sedges

Caddis larva   Sedge pupa   Adult sedge

The food of reservoir trout I (aquatic).

emerger patterns. They are worth utilizing on occasion, but of all the stages of the buzzer they are generally of lesser importance in angling terms.

The empty shuck that is left behind after the pupa hatches would seem to provide very little in the way of nourishment for the trout, and yet the fish feed avidly on them on occasion, as autopsies confirm. Shuck flies (a bit of a misnomer) seem largely to be ignored by anglers, but they do warrant more attention as a fishing strategy and no doubt at some time in the future they will get the recognition that they deserve.

Although there are several patterns tied to represent the winged adults, the returning egg-laying females are but rarely preferred to either the pupae or emerging flies, both of which are around in greater abundance and easier for the trout to catch. Therefore, fishing such artificials is not usually the most productive method.

Daphnia (or water fleas)

The second most important food item of the trout is the humble water flea (not a true flea by the way), which forms vast clouds in the water. The trout eat huge numbers of this crustacean in the same way that whales feed on krill. Being so small it is impossible to imitate them, but fortunately the fish can be caught on virtually anything else when daphnia are on the menu. Orange or peach flies are often recommended, but other flies and methods can be just as killing. Daphnia can be green in colour as well as orange (possibly due to them feeding on green algae) and green flies are probably successful for this reason.

What is important, however, is that the flies are fished *in* the daphnia swarms. The naturals move higher in the water when light levels are low, and retire to deeper water during bright sunlight. This needs to be borne in mind so that the artificials are fished at the correct level. It explains why, to give an example, sometimes it is possible to catch on a longer countdown whereas a shorter one yields nothing. It is because the flies are no longer among the daphnia clouds and therefore are not among the fish feeding on them.

Damsels

In recent years there has been an explosion in the damsel population in reservoirs, just as there has been a diminishing in the number of upwinged flies. This change in populations is probably as a result of ecological changes brought about by fertilizer and pesticide run-off from neighbouring farm land. Imitations of damsel larvae now abound where once there were but few, as fly fishermen have come to realize their great importance in fishing terms.

Where damsels are to be found, which is pretty much anywhere and everywhere, a damsel larva pattern will be a major line of attack all through the year.

Modern damsel imitations, of which there are now dozens, generally seem to be of a more suggestive nature. This would appear to confirm current thinking that such patterns are generally more acceptable than

A fully grown damsel larva that has swum ashore and is ready to emerge.

something of a more precisely imitative character.

Sedges (or caddis flies)

The larvae of caddis flies turn up in autopsies far more regularly than either the pupae or the adult flies, with the largest numbers being seen between April and July. The trout probably find them easy and nourishing pickings as they graze the bed of the reservoir. A sweep of the net will give some idea of the quantity of caddis larvae, which are swallowed case and all, that are available to the fish (*see* illustration in Chapter 15). It is therefore surprising that the number of patterns representing the larvae is so small, whereas there seems to be no shortage of pupae and adult fly imitations.

In the author's experience, sedge pupae very rarely figure in autopsies these days, and they do not warrant much attention from the angler either. A hare's ear pattern could well be taken for a pupa, although it has to be emphasized that it is a minor tactic. I do wonder if trout deliberately avoid sedge pupae and whether the few that are taken are perhaps swallowed by mistake.

An adult sedge fly. Although winged sedges are quite prominent, they turn up in autopsies only infrequently. It is the larvae that are preferred by the trout.

Although they are prominent with their long antennae, adult winged sedges appear in autopsies only occasionally. The G&H Sedge is a successful fly to employ on such occasions. Having said that, it is the author's opinion that it is just as likely to be taken for a trout pellet, which it resembles in shape and colouration, rather than an actual sedge fly. The author used to employ a basic deer hair sedge pattern (simply a deer hair body with a clipped ginger hackle) but felt that it was too much like a trout pellet and so opted for the G&H Sedge, which is no more or less successful, but does salve one's conscience to a small degree.

These deer hair patterns are very useful, however, when their buoyancy is required to keep emergers and other surface flies on the same leader right in, or just under, the surface film. When used in this way the deer hair patterns are frequently taken by the fish, and they appear to be successful whether natural sedges are in evidence or not. Draw your own conclusions!

Water bugs

Under this heading are the corixae, the freshwater or hog louse (not to be confused with fish lice), shrimps, water beetles and various other aquatic creepy-crawlies that inhabit the reservoirs throughout the year.

Autopsies show that these appear in the stomach of the trout on an intermittent basis. There is little evidence to show that trout feed selectively on water bugs, but they do crop up often enough to be considered as part of an all round strategy. The deduction from autopsies could well be that the trout do not actively go out of their way to feed on them, but they are not averse to swallowing them should the occasion arise.

The angler should therefore not ignore the opportunity to fish water bug flies from time to time if autopsies dictate that this is what is needed. If a team of general

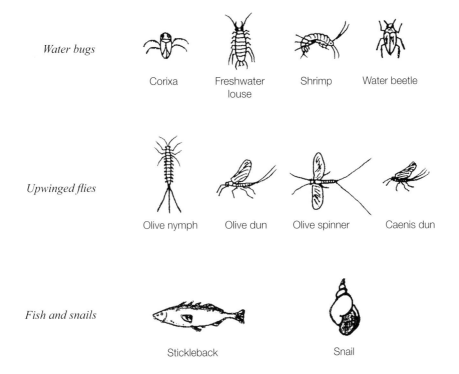

Water bugs — Corixa, Freshwater louse, Shrimp, Water beetle

Upwinged flies — Olive nymph, Olive dun, Olive spinner, Caenis dun

Fish and snails — Stickleback, Snail

The food of reservoir trout II (aquatic).

The corixa (or lesser water boatman).

deceivers is employed, we are probably fishing for them anyway as many of the suggestive patterns, such as the Hare's Ear, Grenadier and Partridge & Silver, could be taken for water bugs.

Secondary Food Items

Upwinged flies (or dayflies)

Sadly, these very beautiful, dainty and delicate insects, once so prolific, seem to be in decline these days. The nymphs are arguably the prettiest of all.

I remember a particular afternoon at Eyebrook Reservoir in the 1970s when a hatch of caenis occurred and it took the appearance of a blizzard – except that the snowflakes were going upwards and not down. Visibility was reduced by the phenomenon and they got everywhere – on your clothes, on your hat, in your eyes, in your ears and in your mouth. As the duns moulted, the empty shucks covered my clothes like hoar frost. I have witnessed nothing on such a grand scale in recent times.

The lake and pond olives show a similar decline. Nevertheless we thankfully still do see them from time to time, although in lesser numbers than in the past. When they do occur, a hare's ear or a pheasant tail, fished around weed beds or in open water, will imitate the nymphs when retrieved with slow draws, twitches and jerks, interspersed with pauses in between to imitate the movement of these 'agile darters' as the nymphs are classified.

The fully grown nymphs hatch and fly away extremely quickly, and as they will have transposed into spinners by the time the females return to lay their eggs, the emergers/duns are of little consequence from an angling point of view.

Olive spinners are taken from time to time, but not in such a quantity that a specific pattern will be required. If you suspect that the trout are taking spent olives, then a general dry pattern such as a Greenwell's Glory or Wickham's Fancy is a good choice.

The caenis, or angler's curse, does not appear in great numbers, as has already been noted (for practical purposes the dun and spinner can be treated as one). When a rise to caenis is taking place, a team of normal-sized deceiver nymphs pulled through any area of activity is probably as likely to get results as endeavouring to use a size 18 imitation to copy them realistically. It will at least offer a better chance of landing the fish should a take be forthcoming.

The larger mayflies are a glorious sight to behold, but they are encountered only

A stunning sight. A mayfly spinner at Eyebrook Reservoir.

infrequently these days. If the angler is fortunate enough to be present when they appear, and they hatch in sufficient numbers to interest the trout, get out the larger nymphs and dry flies and make the most of the opportunity.

Fry and small fish

All reservoirs hold a considerable stock of coarse fish, and trout will feed on their offspring at any time if the opportunity presents itself. In the past, trout fisheries went to great lengths to remove as many coarse fish as possible, but nowadays they

A spectacle that is witnessed all too seldom: mayfly spinners in their pre-nuptial display as they flutter upwards and paraglide down with outstretched tails. Inset: mayfly spinners enlarged.

are accepted as part of the ecological chain and they co-exist with, and provide food for, the trout.

At the back end of the season, starting in August or early September, the trout start fry feeding with a vengeance. The word 'vengeance' is used deliberately, as they can be savage in the way that they decimate the huge shoals of small fish. When the trout attack the shoals of fry that congregate in the margins (and it is generally the larger specimens that will be doing this) it is impossible to see exactly what happens due to the clouds of spray and the leaping fry, but it would appear that the trout charge into the fry to stun them and then return to mop up any dead or injured fish. With the speed of attack it would seem probable that they charge with closed mouths and literally batter the small fish to death. They do not appear to pursue and engulf their quarry in quite the same way that perch do.

An immature stickleback: fry and small fish are a welcome addition to the trout's diet.

107

Lures such as the Appetiser, Missionary, Baby Doll and Jersey Herd, as well as those patterns tied specifically to imitate fish fry, are all suitable representations of small fish when retrieved appropriately.

Weed

This is a strange heading for a book on fly fishing, but vegetable matter does turn up in autopsies on a fairly regular basis. Although it is not suggested that artificial flies should be specifically tied to represent water weed (although there is no reason why they shouldn't), when olive, green and brown flies are fished slowly they could all possibly be taken for underwater foliage of some sort. Generally, weed appears more often in autopsies either early or late on in the season.

Such flies as the GRHE Green Marabou, Olive Grizzle Palmer, Olive Damsel and Dawson's Olive would all appear to be suitable representations of pieces of weed, and if the fish take them when they have weed in their stomach we should not complain.

Minor Tactics

Snails

The migration of the snail population, as they drift in the surface film, is rather like that of lemmings. When trout latch on to snails it may look like a rise to hatching flies, and so correct identification is paramount. A floating snail pattern drifting through with the naturals may be picked up, but sometimes the number of naturals is so vast that the chance of the artificial being taken is much reduced.

Snails are also taken on other occasions, and do turn up in autopsies from time to time, but it is suggested that fishing

An adult alder fly. The author has never found an adult fly in the thousands of autopsies he has carried out, and the alder larva is taken only rarely.

deliberately with snail patterns is not the best use of fishing time.

There are other aquatic creatures that could be mentioned: dragonfly larvae, leeches, aquatic spiders, alder larvae, red mites, phantom larvae and so on, but they are of little consequence from a practical point of view and only tend to confuse the issue. It is only too easy to become side-tracked when unusual items appear. An out of the ordinary autopsy may cause this assertion to be modified, but only rarely.

Terrestrial (or land-bred) insects

We are now getting deep into 'occasional' territory, but land-bred insects do deserve a quick mention. The reader will be familiar with many of the creatures that fall into this category, as they are to be seen in the garden at home as well as at the water-side. When terrestrials are about and are being blown on to the water, and the fish arc sccn to bc taking them, is one of the few occasions when a relatively close copy dry or partially submerged artificial can be profitable.

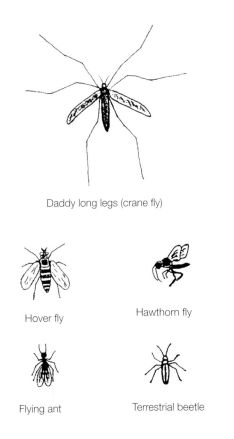

Daddy long legs (crane fly)

Hover fly

Hawthorn fly

Flying ant

Terrestrial beetle

The food of reservoir trout III (terrestrials).

Of all the terrestrials listed in this section, by far the most important is the daddy long legs, which in a good season (for them) will hatch in sufficiently large numbers to interest the trout if the breeze is sufficient to blow these gangly and poor fliers out onto the lake. When the trout lock on to them is one of the times when they may feed selectively. On occasion a trout can be so full of daddies that the spooning will literally resemble a ball of shredded wheat, which will only reveal its true nature when the contents are placed in a dish of water and the mass separates.

In those years when daddies are seen in any great number it is wise to position oneself on the bank, or anchor the boat, where the offshore wind is taking the flies out to the waiting fish and to cast an artificial (well treated with floatant) into the general area of activity. Surprisingly, when the fish are taking such flies from the surface they will also take them submerged just below the surface film as well, and they seem to make little distinction between the two. It follows, therefore, that if the fly sinks, rather than pulling it in immediately it may be wise to retrieve slowly in the hope that a trout will take it. Some seasons will produce a good number of daddies, whereas other years will only yield a small number. If the season is a poor one, the fish will be less likely to show a great deal of interest in them. Observation, as ever, is of paramount importance.

Imitations of other terrestrials are useful at their specific times, but it has to be emphasized that such occasions will be

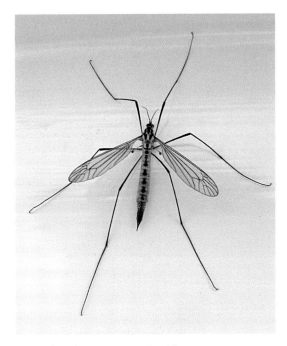

Daddy long legs are a considerable mouthful for any trout.

*When there is a fall of hover flies it
can bring about a general rise.*

infrequent. Nevertheless, every angler
should possess a few passable imitations
of the terrestrials listed in the table below
in his dry fly box ready for the appropriate occasion. Some years they may not be
required, but on those occasions that do
demand their use, nothing else will probably be quite so successful.

Emergence dates of terrestrial insects

Insect	Emergence (very approx.)
Daddy long legs (crane fly)	From August (occasionally before)
Hover fly (or drone fly) (occasionally)	Summer
Hawthorn fly	End April/early May
Flying ant (often a once-a-year experience)	From mid summer
Terrestrial beetle	Any time

The table covers all the land-bred insects
that may reasonably be expected, and it is
wise not to confuse matters by including
all the rarer possibilities such as cowdung
flies, grasshoppers, black gnats, spiders,
moths, lacewings and so on, which sometimes appear in textbooks. They rarely
occur in sufficient numbers to interest the
fish and cause a rise, and so they can be
safely ignored.

Conclusion

This chapter has covered all the items
that the trout feed on to any substantial
degree, and there are surely more than
enough here for practical angling purposes. Detailed analysis of my records of
autopsies over the last few years showed
that six food items accounted for more
than 95 per cent of everything found
inside a typical reservoir trout. The results
were perhaps not surprising and were, in
order of preference:

1   buzzer pupae,
2   daphnia,
3   bloodworm,
4   damsel larvae,
5   caddis larvae,
6   water bugs.

Apart from those occasions when the
trout are known to be taking a season-
ally abundant item, or when an autopsy
reveals something else, the angler who
sets out to fish deceivers that suggest the
above would probably not go far wrong.
The table opposite summarizes what can
be expected to be found in autopsies, and
at what time of year they will be of greatest
importance.

Aquatic items frequently found in autopsies throughout the season

	March	April	May	June	July	Aug	Sept	Oct
Bloodworm	☑	✓	✓	✓	☑	☑	✓	☑
Buzzer pupa	✓✓	✓✓	✓✓	✓✓	✓✓	✓	✓✓	✓✓
Buzzer shuck		✓	☑	☑	☑		✓	✓
Buzzer adult							✓	
Daphnia		✓✓	✓✓	✓✓	✓✓	✓✓	✓✓	✓✓
Damsel larva		✓	✓	✓	☑	☑	☑	
Caddis larva		✓	✓	✓	☑			
Sedge pupa								
Adult sedge								
Water bugs	☑	✓	✓	✓		☑	✓	✓
Olive nymph			☑					
Olive spinner								
Caenis dun/spinner								
Fry						✓	✓	✓
Snail								
Weed		✓	☑				✓	✓

Abundant items = ✓✓. Frequent items = ✓. Occasional items = ☑. All other items rarely.

The above are what can most commonly be expected to be found in autopsies. This does not necessarily illustrate what the angler may observe around him at the waterside! It is intended to show what food forms are likely to prove to be the most successful, but, as always, modifications should be made as autopsies, observation and local conditions dictate.

A General Rule to Follow

A general rule to follow concerning those items that appear occasionally is that if they do not appear more than once in any particular autopsy they are probably of insufficient importance to warrant specific imitation and should therefore be dismissed from practical consideration.

The author has an interest in entomology, hence his close attention to spoonings and the identification of what is found, but in many ways this is a completely different pastime and care has to be taken not to be sidetracked into blind alleys that are unnecessary and counterproductive for a fly fisherman.

11 Tactics

Now that the practicalities of tackle selection and its use have been considered, the location of where the trout might be has been decided, and the food that the trout will probably be targeting has been studied, it is time to see how this can help when out on the reservoir bank.

Hunting a wild quarry such as a trout necessitates having a well-formulated plan of campaign to outwit them, rather than simply arriving at the water without any strategic objective and applying random guesswork made up on the spur of the moment. All the effort expended so far would have been of little value if it did not help to make our fishing more pleasurable and ultimately more successful but, as we shall shortly see, the time and trouble taken will prove to have been worthwhile. The success or failure of any endeavour is often determined at the planning and preparation stage, and in this regard fly fishing is no different.

Choice of Flies

Perhaps the most important dilemma every fly angler has to resolve satisfactorily is which fly is to be tied on to the end of the leader and how it is to be fished. It is essential to choose the right fly, not only to attract the fish but also to give the angler confidence in what he is doing.

Regrettably, all too often fly choice is based on either mere arbitrary whim, the selection of patterns that have been successful for the angler previously (although not necessarily in the same conditions), those that have been recommended by other anglers, the currently fashionable ones in the angling press, those that look appealing in the fly box, or just pot luck! None of these methods will ever give confidence and assurance, and yet the majority of successful anglers would agree that confidence is an indefinable attribute that seems to stretch right down the rod to the fish and induce success.

In simple terms, if the angler is able to choose patterns that the fish recognize as something that they should take, the battle is already half won. This is why identifying the food items that the trout are feeding on, and then replicating them, is as essential as it is straightforward and why it has been dealt with in such detail in preceding chapters. If this information is known, the angler will have a good idea of what flies to choose, and be able to make his selection with a degree of confidence. The tables in Chapters 10 and 14 have been devised to assist in the selection of a fly that replicates the size, colour and form of the natural to some degree.

The range of flies recommended in Chapter 14 should form the basis of a good all round selection from which it is possible to select a fly to cope with most eventualities without being so all encompassing that the array is baffling. In addition to these, a small assortment of lures and perhaps some locally successful flies will complete the collection. Local favourites are popular because they

A stunning 2lb 8oz rainbow from Ringstead Grange Fishery. After a fine tussle with such a well-conditioned and fully finned fish, it is no wonder that the author looks so happy.

are successful, and so it is unwise to dismiss them. However, an element of caution should be exercised, rather than pinning one's faith blindly on something that might not be appropriate on the day.

It is inevitable that over time other flies will make their way into the fly boxes, and it is up to the angler to prune them to manageable proportions when necessary.

Retrieve Methods to Match the Naturals

Once the flies have been chosen, the next step is to attempt to fish them in a way that is appropriate to the creature they are intended to represent. In the same way that exaggerated features in artificial flies seem to appeal to the fish more than a straightforward 'carbon copy', so a style of retrieve that exaggerates the movement of the natural seems to be more acceptable to the fish. It could be that a more pronounced retrieve stands out from the host of naturals around it, or it could be because it simulates the frenzied flight of a nymph as it endeavours to elude capture by a predator.

The table opposite indicates the chief food items of the trout, where they are commonly to be found and how they behave as they move in the water. Replicating the movement of the relevant creatures gives a valid starting point upon which to build, and as fishing progresses the angler should work around this until a successful taking method has been found.

It is difficult to describe accurately on paper the way that many of the creatures move around, and probably the best way to comprehend this is for the reader to procure a clear container that is filled with lake water and stocked with a few specimens collected at the waterside. How they behave and react can then be observed at first hand, and the time doing this will be well spent.

Studying nymphs, bugs and larvae at leisure in their own surroundings will not only help the angler to move his imitations in a more lifelike manner, it is a fascinating exercise in its own right, which teaches much about life under the surface and will give a deeper understanding and appreciation of the environment that the trout inhabit.

Tactics for Fishing

When it comes to casting our flies at the fish it is necessary to have our enquiring mindset operating once more. Rather than methodically going through the motions, fishing every cast the same monotonous way, every cast should be an enquiry. Do the fish want the flies presented this way? Or do they want them presented differently?

After a few casts the approach should be varied by counting down the flies after touchdown for longer or shorter periods to try to determine the level the fish are at until eventually contact is made. The method and speed of retrieve should be altered, permuting all the options until we finally hit upon where the fish are and how they want it.

Fanning out each successive cast enables slightly different areas of water to be fished

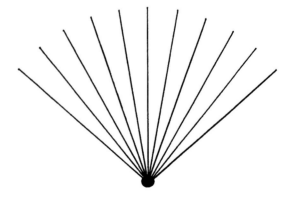

Fanning the casts. Twenty-five-yard casts at 10 degrees to each other will land 4.4yd apart.

Food items of the trout: where located and the manner of movement

Food item	Location	Description of movement
Bloodworm	Bottom in shallow and deep water; also free swimming in mid water	Wriggling motion
Buzzer pupa (1)	Bottom, mid water and subsurface	Jerky or wriggling
Buzzer pupa (2)	Just below and in surface film	Jerky, or stationary hatching
Buzzer shuck	In surface film	None, drifts with current
Buzzer adult	Surface	Stationary, or dipping★
Daphnia	Mid water or subsurface	Tiny jerks, drifts with current
Damsel larva (1)	Bottom in shallow and medium-depth water	Slow wiggling walk, crawling, or wriggling swimming
Damsel larva (2)	Subsurface	Wriggling swimming
Caddis larva	Bottom in shallow and medium-depth water	Agile crawling
Sedge pupa	Bottom, mid water, subsurface	Swimming or hatching†
Adult sedge	On surface	Swift progress often causing a 'V' wake, or dipping★
Corixa	Shallow water	Very jerky
Freshwater louse	Bottom in shallow or medium-depth water	Busy, slithering, creeping motion
Shrimp	Shallow and medium-depth water	Jerky, swimming on side
Water beetle	Shallow and medium-depth water	Jerky swimming
Olive nymph	Shallow and medium-depth water	Darting with pauses
Olive spinner	On surface and in surface film	Dipping★, or stationary spent
Caenis dun/spinner	On surface and in surface film	Little movement, or stationary spent
Fry	Shallow water	Swift darting with pauses, or stationary
Snail	In weed beds Beneath surface film	None visible Drifting with current
Weed	Shallow and medium-depth water	Stationary or drifting

★'Dipping' describes the behaviour of flying egg-laying females as they skim the surface to deposit their eggs.
†Hatching sedges can cause a considerable disturbance.

each time, water that has not been previously fished or disturbed. A difference in angle of 10 degrees between each successive cast will, in due course, enable us to cover every fish within casting range of our fishing position. If I remember the geometry I learnt at school correctly, a variation of 10 degrees over a 25yd cast will mean that the flies land almost 4½yd apart from the previous attempt.

Fishing at an angle to the wind as opposed to directly downwind is generally the more profitable method, as fish moving upwind will see more of the flies because they are in profile, rather than just a rear view. In addition, delivering the fly line at an angle allows the wind to blow a floating line across in an arc, which will hopefully drift the flies across the fish's nose. When casting straight downwind the line has nowhere to go, apart from any movement made by the current, and it can only be pulled straight in.

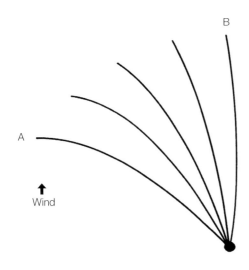

Drift of line cast at an angle to the wind.
Line cast to 'A' drifts round to 'B'.

It is not unusual for the fish always to come from one particular segment and for other areas to be less profitable. Once this segment has been established it is possible to concentrate on the productive area.

If we get a few plucks or other indications, but no actual takes, it is time to alter things slightly in order to provoke a more positive response. A smaller fly may be necessary, or a jerkier retrieve, or a faster retrieve, but always vary things and seek to find the optimum method for the day.

It is vital to memorize precisely what each cast consisted of, as in the excitement of hooking and playing a fish it is all too easy to forget what was being done beforehand. Once the killing method has been established, this must be replicated if we want to catch more of the same. It is essential to try and remember both the countdown time and the method of retrieve employed just before the 'take'. It is not an easy thing to do whilst concentrating hard on the line, looking for signs of the fish and generally taking in what is happening on the water, but it is crucial.

If, on the other hand, there is nothing doing and there has been no response after 20 or 30min then either:

- The trout are not there, in which case it is time to think about moving. Whether on the bank or in the boat, the same applies.
- We are fishing at the wrong depth, in which case it is time to alter the countdown dramatically, exchange the fly for a weighted one, change the braided or polymer leader being used, or else change the fly line to one with a different sink rate.
- We are not giving them what they want and should consider whether changing the pattern of fly is appropriate.

Braided and Polymer Leaders

When attempting to get the depth just right we have a valuable asset that we can employ – the variations in sink rate offered by the use of the different densities of braided and polymer leaders. For example, by using a similar density to the fly line the retrieve will be in a horizontal plane, whereas by using a fast sinking one with, say, an intermediate line we get a sink tip effect and can 'sink and draw' the flies. The permutations are endless, and it is up to the angler to decide what he wants to do. He can then select the leader density that will most closely achieve the required effect.

As in all things, experiment and change until success comes. Do not take the easy but unthinking option of flogging away at the same method in the vain hope that your 'luck' will change. A fish may well take, but we have to ask whether it is unnecessarily restricting our chances.

However, once we hit on 'the' method we can repeat it and hopefully catch further fish until either we want a fresh challenge and move off somewhere else and start again, or alternatively the fish move on or change their feeding habits and we stop catching, in which case the searching process has to be started again.

How many times have we started fishing at one particular spot and not had any offer and then subsequently moved position and 'bagged up' in a relatively short period of time? Staying in one place all day could result in a blank. If the fish are not there, move on.

On those occasions when things are not going our way, it is sometimes wise to stop fishing and have a cup of coffee and think things through slowly and logically. Very often during these breaks an idea will formulate itself in the mind and we will start once again with renewed concentration, conviction and vigour – and the fish may begin to co-operate.

Some Typical Fishing Scenarios

Successful fly fishing is all about formulating a plan of action that takes into account all the salient features of the chosen fishing location, the prevailing conditions, and the mood of the fish. Because these are so variable, no two sets of circumstances will be exactly the same. Nevertheless, similar scenarios do recur on a regular basis and some examples will be examined in more detail. It is stressed that the following scenarios are only generalizations, and it is up to the individual to experiment and modify each one until the taking method has been discovered.

Nymph fishing in shallow water

This is probably the most commonly employed method of fishing deceivers; it can be used from the bank or the boats and it is straightforward and can be very successful. Nevertheless, in spite of the simplicity of the method it is important to give careful thought before coming to a decision about which flies to use and how they are to be fished. A team of small nymphs will probably be chosen, and at the appropriate time they can be imitations of practically every form of food that the trout are likely to ingest. The flies are cast and retrieved around weed beds, any features (see 'Where in the reservoir are the fish?' in Chapter 8) or other likely looking spots, or into open water.

The depth that the flies are fishing, the speed and the manner of retrieve are all varied until the fish begin to co-operate. For maximum sensitivity the rod is pointed straight down the line and takes are felt by the pads of the fingers. Nymph fishing like this is arguably the most interesting fly fishing method of all, and when used appropriately it can be the most successful one as well.

Nymph fishing in deep water

Once deeper water is encountered, any weed beds will start to thin out due to the absence of light, and hence the presence of those creatures that rely on water plants for food and shelter will also start to decline. Fishing will, in the main, be from a boat (or possibly the dam wall) and if the fish are not feeding in the surface layers there will be three primary lines of attack.

The first approach is to fish in mid water where daphnia will probably be present in vast numbers as well as ascending buzzers and other actively swimming nymphs. Patterns to replicate these will be fished using a figure of eight retrieve. As the depth of water increases, the flies may need to be increased in hook size, and as well as nymphs the larger general-purpose marabou flies can be utilized to good effect.

Using the second approach, the flies will be fished hard on the bottom (if it is clean) or just above the weed (if any is present) using bloodworm, buzzer pupae, caddis larvae, damsel larvae and similar imitations. It is important to remember that trout will not take flies that are weeded and so noting the countdown time and finding out how deep the flies can descend, but without catching on weed, will enable the flies to be fished in the right location. Once the right depth has been discovered, it will be necessary to fish the flies slowly to ensure that they do not rise in the water.

A third method is to use an ultra fast sinking line with nymph patterns in the dropper positions and a booby on the point. The flies will fish quite deeply but the buoyancy of the booby will keep the flies above the fly line and prevent them from snagging the bottom. This method needs to be fished slowly.

Fishing from points

When bank fishing, it is usually more advantageous to fish from points rather than in bays as they are generally more productive;

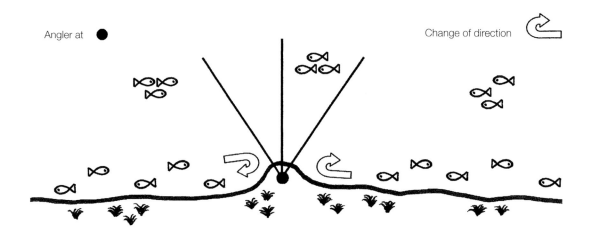

Fishing from a 'point'.

there are sound reasons for this. Firstly, points usually give access to deeper water whereas bays tend to be shallower. Trout appear to patrol long stretches of the bank, but once they arrive at a point they will often turn around and retrace their course rather than move to a different depth. This means that the angler not only has the fish within his casting area for a longer period of time, but he is also fishing for three different groups of fish – those approaching from the left, those approaching from the right, and those straight ahead.

We do not know all the reasons why points are as productive as they are, but it is a fact that trout cruise in the vicinity of them and so they should be fished whenever the occasion presents itself. Having said that, such spots are more likely to be taken up first!

Bank fishing in early season

This can be one of the most productive parts of the season for the bank angler, as the trout will often be congregating in the margins in large numbers. At the appropriate time the results from the bank can beat those from the boats. If the fish are feeding hard to pack on weight and condition after the winter months, which they often are in March and April, a team of slowly fished nymphs can deliver the goods. If they are not feeding, and on occasion autopsies will reveal nothing inside the fish, it may be advantageous to try large marabou nymphs fished slowly but with life and movement, or alternatively lures fished fast.

Drifting the flies with the wind

One of the most enjoyable and successful methods for the bank angler is possible when a preferably left to right breeze (for a right hander) allows the angler to drift the flies round with the wind. The procedure is to cast the flies ahead and slightly to the right, and the action of the wind on the floating line carries the line and flies slowly round in a 90-degree arc, which eventually finishes up parallel to the bank. During this time just sufficient line is retrieved to keep in contact

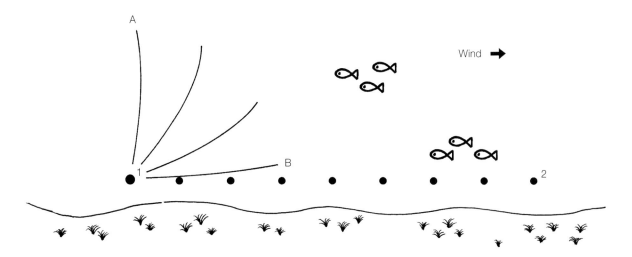

Drifting flies with the wind. Line cast to 'A' swings round to 'B'. Angler moves down bank from ●¹ to ●².

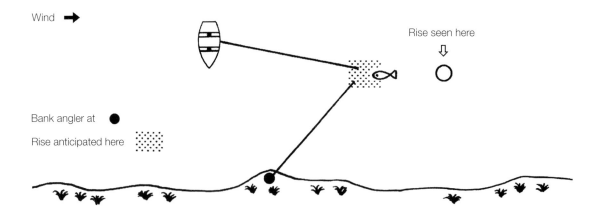

Casting to rising fish. Trout will generally be swimming upwind.

with the flies, but not actually move them, and longer and shorter casts enable large tracts of water to be covered. Fish can be taken at any point during the 'retrieve'.

If the banks are clear of other anglers, it is possible to move a few paces down the bank after a few casts and fish new water each time until the trout are located. When the fish are taking ascending buzzers or other hatching nymphs, this method can (almost) be guaranteed to produce a fish or two, and takes at such times will often be firm and confident.

Casting to rising fish

One of the most exciting sights any fly fisher can witness is a rising trout; when this happens within casting range the angler should have a go and cast to it. It is a question of lifting off and casting quickly and accurately – but at the same time endeavouring not to disturb the fish. The flies (but never the fly line) should be delivered as close to the fish as possiblc, and if thcy are not taken almost immediately then a couple of steady draws (when fishing wet flies) may well attract the trout's attention.

Once a trout has risen the problem is guessing where it will rise next time! Trout that are on the move near the surface tend to swim upwind so that any food will be blown towards them, as opposed to chasing food that is being blown away from them downwind. When the trout are actively swimming, and sometimes they will be swimming quite fast, the flies should be placed slightly ahead of the spot where the next rise is expected to be. With fish that are rising in the same place every time things are much simpler, and the angler should attempt to land the tail fly right in the ring of the rise.

Sometimes the fish do not take a fly that is cast directly to them, and under such circumstances, or if the angler prefers a more leisurely approach, either leaving a static team of flies for the trout to find or alternatively retrieving them slowly through the general area of activity may produce results.

The occasions when angling for visibly rising fish is successful must be one of the most rewarding any fly angler can have; when a fast and accurate throw results in a satisfying 'clunk' at the other end and a lively feeding fish is 'on'! The fish has been hunted, it has been deceived, and it has been caught.

Flat calms

During flat calms everything should be done more slowly and quietly so that any disturbance and line wake are eliminated. Using a slow intermediate line instead of a floater, fishing smaller flies as fine as possible, and degreasing the leader regularly so that it does not break the surface (which it has a habit of doing when the surface tension is greater) may all be advantageous.

If flat calms are accompanied by very clear water the difficulties can be multiplied, but nevertheless, with a little thought and a lot of care, large bags are achievable. Under such conditions, although the angler may be more visible to the fish and he therefore needs to take extra precautions, the fish are also more visible to the angler, and hence it is possible to see where they are and how they are behaving.

Bright sunshine, hot temperatures, no breeze and warm water

These conditions can often be very difficult for the fly angler and it is as well to be realistic and accept that large bags are less likely. Probably the wisest course of action is to make the best of things, enjoy the 'nice' weather, and try as many different methods as possible until an approach that will take a fish or two is found. This is when possessing a wide range of techniques will pay off.

Bank fishing will probably be out of the question because the fish will usually be in the deeps, but from the boats it is at least possible to get over the fish, which is half the problem solved, and to aim for a brace (anything else should be regarded as a bonus) rather than a limit. Static or back-drifted boobies fished on the bottom, or buzzers and other nymphs drifted round on a long leader over deep water (perhaps under an indicator) may be the best lines of attack; but slowly retrieved nymphs, or perhaps a flashy lure fished fast, may all be tried until a response is obtained. Trout can be very unpredictable and against all the odds the fish sometimes do co-operate during such weather and a limit can be taken – but don't bank on it!

Once things start to cool down in the evening the fish may well come to the top and start to rise, in which case other techniques, including fishing dries, can be tried.

The evening rise

The eagerly anticipated evening rise does not always materialize quite as expected, but on those occasions when it does it can either prove to be a profitable time or on occasion an exceedingly frustrating one. The classic scenario is when, as evening progresses, a few rises are seen (usually well beyond casting range) and as the light starts to fail more and more rises occur, coming closer and closer and intensifying from gentle sips, to slurps, and then sloshes. Fishing a team of buzzer pupae or nymphs very slowly, dry flies, or using 'wet and dry' methods can all prove successful, but on occasion the fish will rise all around but seldom fall to an artificial. On occasion a fish is caught in the last few minutes before packing up. If sedges are about they may well be more conspicuous, but autopsies will often reveal that buzzers are being preferred.

Indicator fishing

Fishing a team of flies under an indicator (in reality a float!) has become a commonly used and accepted method, and numerous indicators made of yarn, foam, putty and buoyant plastic are on sale nowadays. Usually a team of buzzers or nymphs is

Home at dusk with the reward for an afternoon fishing against the odds in hot, bright and still conditions: eight trout caught in less than 3hr on a team of buzzers drifted round on a 20ft leader.

Fishing the evening rise.

suspended below the indicator, with the heaviest fly being placed on the point to keep everything straight. The whole lot is cast out and the angler simply keeps in touch and waits for something to happen. Sometimes the indicator will move, tremble or dip slightly before finally submerging completely, and the angler tightens up in response. Alternatively, if the angler is not paying attention, the fish takes line until a pull is felt. It can be a productive method, but it does not seem as though the angler is 'working' for his fish. Hence many will find that it is not a particularly stimulating or satisfying way of fishing.

Booby fishing on the bottom

At those times when the fish are hard on the bottom and other methods are not producing, a booby fished on the reservoir bed on an ultra fast sinker will sometimes work. A single fly is employed on a very short leader, from 12in to 36in, so that the fly rises just above the lake floor. The line is cast as far as possible and is allowed to sink to the bottom, which can take a couple of minutes or more in deep water, and either left static or slowly retrieved with short pulls with pauses in between, causing the fly to be pulled down and then rise again under its own buoyancy.

Takes can be very firm, and trout caught on boobies tend to swallow the fly and be deeply hooked. For this reason the method cannot be used with catch and release.

It is not particularly interesting fishing, but on dour days when nothing else is getting a response it can be used as a last resort, although once a couple of fish are in the bag, the thinking angler will probably want to return to more traditional fly fishing methods.

Stripping muddlers and boobies in the waves

Stripping a muddler or a booby through the waves can be an exciting (and produc-tive) method. A breezy day with a ripple is required and the flies are stripped at high speed, causing a pronounced wake, or else retrieved so that they bounce from wave crest to wave crest.

A floating line is ideal, used with a leader of around 10ft, with or without a single dropper carrying a size 8 or 10 mini lure or nymph 4ft away from the point fly. The trout will either take the muddler or booby, or will approach it and turn away taking the dropper fly on the way down. The theory is that the setup represents the muddler (or booby) chasing the smaller fly, and it entices the trout to snap it up before the muddler is able to do so; whether or not that is the trout's perception of things is not

With a brisk onshore wind a band of muddy water stretches out into Pitsford Reservoir.

certain, but it works! It is not particularly sophisticated fishing, but the fish take with a wallop so that strong leaders in the order of 10lb BS are recommended.

Muddy edge feeders

When a strong wind is blowing onshore and stirring up the margins, it is often the case that a band of muddied water will run along the bank extending for several yards out into the body of the reservoir, but ending quite abruptly with a clearly defined edge where clearer water further out predominates (this is especially so when the wind is blowing onshore and along the bank).

The trout patrol the clear water next to the edge, waiting for creatures that have been washed out of the bank or reservoir bed to venture out into the clear water where they are clearly visible (and edible).

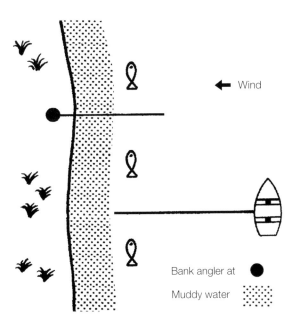

Muddy edge feeders.

Tackling these fish can be done from the bank or from a boat, but the bank angler is at a distinct advantage in that both he and his tackle are screened from the fish by the curtain of opaque water. Drifting a team of nymphs along the edge in the clear water can be profitable.

End-of-season fry feeders

As the back end of the season approaches, vast shoals of fry start to congregate in the shallows, and the trout find them rich pickings. The best places to locate fry are around any features such as the boat dock or the corner of the dam, where the marauding trout may well betray themselves by violent swirls; the clouds of fry leaping to escape are another giveaway. Although the fish may seem to be in a feeding frenzy, they are nevertheless wary and difficult to catch.

Patterns such as a Cat's Whisker, White Tadpole, Minkie or Muddler Minnow pulled through any area of activity may be taken by the trout as they herd the small fry preparatory to devouring them. Alternatively, a static Floating Fry tied to represent an unconscious, injured, dying or sick fish can be left stationary on the surface, or occasionally gently twitched to provoke interest as the trout work the margins.

Fishing for fry feeders from the bank at the back end of the season can be exciting, and the tension that builds up as the trout approaches and we speculate whether or not it will take our offering is beyond words. If we are successful, it can result in the largest fish of the season, possibly even a specimen brownie, being landed.

Fishing a single fly is recommended, and a powerful rod and line combination (maybe a no. 9) may be necessary to cast the larger flies (anything from a size 2 longshank to a size 8) customarily used. It is important

Brian Calvert plays a lively fry-feeding trout in front of the lodge at Grafham Water. (Photo courtesy of Anglian Water Hooked *magazine – Cliff Waters.)*

to locate the fry to gauge how big they are and then employ a similarly sized artificial. Travel light and keep on the move; if an individual fish does not want to know do not educate it but leave it alone and come back later when its confidence has returned and have another try.

The foregoing are a few typical scenarios of many, but the approaches outlined should not be followed blindly. Beware the mental attitude that says, 'this is situation A and so method A should be employed'. Even when we are getting an offer every 20min it is still possible to modify things so that we get one every 10min!

Keeping a Fishing Diary

Having gone to all the trouble of finding out what was successful, it would be a great shame if the information and experience gained were subsequently lost and forgotten. In years gone by the keeping of fishing diaries was a commonplace exercise. It is one that is now largely neglected, but it can prove invaluable for future reference.

A fishing diary should provide the maximum information for the least amount of effort. A systematic approach to recording is needed, and a hardback record book or card index system will be best. In recent years the author has been using purpose-designed record cards photocopied on to A5 160gsm white card, which contain all the appropriate columns and boxes to be completed; in this way nothing can be overlooked. They are filed in date (but not year) order in a card index box, so that it is easy to look up a particular time of year and make comparisons. It is suggested that something durable is used, as they do tend to get well thumbed as time goes by.

A copy of the author's record card is illustrated in Appendix III. It can be amended to suit the requirements of individual anglers. The record card should be uncomplicated, so that it can be written up in a few minutes the same evening from brief notes that are made at the waterside on pieces of card carried for the purpose. It is easy to forget exactly what occurred if it is put off until later. Should we go out again in similar conditions, it is a simple matter to look up what happened before and see what was successful.

A 'trout fishing' photograph album kept in conjunction with the fishing record is both interesting and useful. Pictures of the water fished and its surrounding countryside, the local wildlife, of autopsies, of other anglers met on the bank (ask their permission first), and any interesting features that have been observed, as well as the catches of trout can be included. Referring back to these records in the dark winter months can bring back memories that could otherwise be forgotten.

12 Bank Fishing and Boat Fishing

When it comes down to fishing tactics it makes sense to be where the fish are, and any angler should make sure that his chances are not being hampered unnecessarily by being on the bank when the fish are 400yd away in the middle of the reservoir. Conversely, there is no point in fishing in the middle when the trout are in the margins.

In early season the banks are probably the place to be, and it is relatively easy to be among fish that are feeding hard and which, as yet, are unaware of the danger from humans. As the season progresses and the margins become more heavily weeded and the fish have moved offshore, it is then sensible to go afloat and follow the fish until conditions again dictate otherwise.

There is a comradeship between bank anglers that makes fishing there enjoyable, and if you are among a bunch of anglers who are willing to chat and exchange ideas as well as fish together, and who have a sense of humour as well, it can make a good day even better. In contrast, when in the boats, which by their very nature are a much more solitary occupation, you cannot stroll up to other anglers and either congratulate or commiserate with them as appropriate. In fact, if you motored up to talk you would probably be told to clear off and quite rightly too!

Bank or Boat

Whether fishing from the bank or from a boat, in basic terms they are both simply fishing platforms from which to cast and retrieve. Nevertheless, they do have some fundamental differences.

Fishing from a boat generally seems to be the domain of the fly fisher rather than the coarse angler who normally tends to fish from the bank. It stands to reason therefore that most coarse anglers who have turned to trout fishing will probably know little of boat handling, and yet proficient boat management does contribute towards success.

All of the waters of the size we are considering offer bank fishing, nearly all allow wading, and most probably they will have a fleet of boats for hire, which gives three different options from which to choose:

1 Bank fishing: Static position – from the bank or wading in the margins.
2 Anchored boat: Static position.
3 Drifting boat: Moving position.

Bank Fishing

On virtually all reservoirs, wading is allowed in most places, apart from the dam wall, and as a consequence the majority of anglers will probably be wading if the contours allow. Although it is possible to catch fish in shallow undisturbed water close to the bank without resorting to wading, if other anglers wade then to have any chance of reaching the fish it will usually be necessary to follow suit and wade, because the disturbance they will have caused will have driven the fish further out. Many anglers do not know how to wade quietly, or else simply do not care whether they make a commotion or not, and that makes things difficult for everybody.

Wading in reservoirs is a procedure where care should be exercised. Providing it is done carefully, by making sure that one foot is firmly planted on firm ground before moving the other one, all should be well. Using the landing net handle as a wading staff is a wise precaution if the terrain is unfamiliar. When fishing a new water it is

a good idea to ask the warden if there are any areas that are precarious and should be treated with caution or avoided altogether. Some quite innocuous-looking areas can be akin to quicksand! Slipping over, even in quite shallow water, can be a frightening and even a dangerous experience.

Wading can be a pleasant occupation providing the angler is well organized with all the necessary tackle close to hand, and it does allow deeper water to be reached than would otherwise be possible. Once in the chosen fishing position it is imperative to be able to perform all the necessary tasks whilst standing in the water, without constantly having to wade ashore to change flies, degrease the leader, or perform any of the basic tasks that are required. Wading in and out only disturbs the fish and may well push them beyond casting range, at least for a while. Be organized and have everything

A successful evening's work from the bank. Five rainbows taken on a floating line and buzzer pupae imitations drifted with the wind.

to hand. Having tackle attached to zingers will ensure that it will not get dropped into the water.

When it is absolutely necessary to come ashore, perhaps for lunch or a coffee break, or to dispatch and spoon a fish (it is not essential to come ashore to do this), it should be done slowly and quietly, with as little commotion and as few ripples as possible.

The format of searching out the water, as previously discussed, should be carried out, and if all attempts fail, move on. It is no use sticking to one spot, however well it may have produced in the past, and however pleasant it might seem, if the fish are elsewhere.

The dread of every wading angler occurs when he attempts to go in just that little bit too far and just that little bit too deep; the inevitable happens – water seeps over the tops of the waders and the result is a wet leg and a soggy groin for the rest of the day. Not a particularly enjoyable or uplifting experience.

Fishing from the dam walls, if it is allowed, can be hazardous, especially when the surfaces are wet and slippery; the wearing of non-slip footwear rather than waders is a sensible precaution. Wading from the dam walls is not safe and is quite sensibly prohibited.

Boat Fishing

To the uninitiated, being in a small boat floating in the middle of 500 acres of water that is 40 feet deep with the nearest

The boat dock at Rutland Water. Anglers travel far and wide to fish the most prestigious trout fishery in Europe.

bank maybe a half a mile away may seem like a daunting prospect and an unsafe one too. To reassure those who have never ventured out in one, modern boats are very stable if used correctly, and they are virtually unsinkable even if they are holed or they overturn (an occurrence which should never happen if one is careful). The fibre-glass boats usually employed almost invariably have moulded-in buoyancy tanks.

The boats in use today are either rowing boats, which are usually confined to the smaller waters, or else powered by petrol outboard motors. On the largest waters, motor boats are the only ones in use nowadays as the distances to be covered would take far too long and would exhaust the batteries of any electric motor, let alone a rower.

Petrol outboard motors tend to be quite easy to start these days and give few problems even to those who are not mechanically minded. If one is able to start and use a petrol lawnmower then an outboard motor will not pose any great difficulty. If it is unfamiliar in any way, ask the fishery attendant for instructions and to give a demonstration.

Where rowing boats are the only option for hire it is usual to allow the angler to bring his own electric motor with him and screw it to the boat. If a lot of such fishing is envisaged, the purchase of one's own motor is well worth considering if funds permit. Unless you are very fit a day's rowing will be exhausting, whereas getting around with an electric motor is effortless once the motor and battery (both quite heavy) have been carried down to the boat. Electric outboard motors cost in the region of £250 upwards, and the leisure batteries to power them (it is as well to have a spare) will cost about £50 each. Keeping the batteries fully charged at all times will require a trickle charger, and this should

be connected up and switched on immediately after returning home. Looking after the battery and checking the electrolyte levels regularly pays dividends in lasting peak power and prolonged battery life.

Being Organized Pays Dividends

One word of advice, a boat is a small place in which to be confined for a whole day (surrounded by fragile tackle, heavy anchors, cumbersome oars, wet drogues and hefty wellington boots), and so great care is needed. Before casting off make sure that everything is tidy and carefully stowed away, and ensure that all rod tips are kept well within the confines of the boat when both casting off and finally docking. That way nothing should get broken.

If you are proposing to fish with a partner, make sure you will get on together; a boat is very small indeed if things go sour. The day, and possibly a friendship, could be spoiled if the choice is an unwise one. The great benefit of having two anglers in the boat is that each is able to try a different method until the fish have been located. Once this happens, the unsuccessful angler then changes his tackle set-up and tactics to the taking method and they (hopefully) both start catching.

The author prefers to fish alone most of the time, because then you have no one else to consult about where to fish, before moving, about changing tactics, when to have lunch, or even calling it a day. Some anglers, on the other hand, prefer fishing with a friend.

Boat Safety

The two principle hazards to avoid when boat fishing are overturning the boat and falling over the side. Both can be virtually eliminated with a little thought and care. Falling in generally occurs when getting

Ready for the off! Everything has been stowed away carefully.

into or out of the boat and so taking extra care is wise.

The use of a lifejacket has already been discussed in the section on tackle in Chapter 3, but the advice already given is worth repeating: *never go afloat without wearing a lifejacket at all times*. Some anglers take a lifejacket with them and then simply leave it in the bottom of the boat in case of bad weather, which is most unwise.

When the wind is light the possibility of turning the boat over is small, but when the wind increases the chances are multiplied.

Keep the weight evenly distributed throughout the boat. If the angler is fishing alone, any heavy gear should be stowed at the bows, with the angler either fishing amidships or seated at the tiller (the handle that controls the rudder and throttle) when moving. When two anglers are fishing the same rule applies, and they should be located at either end of the boat. Although the bows are the wettest place to be when motoring into the wind in very

rough conditions, it is by far the safest way of maintaining boat stability. Safety should take precedence over comfort!

In high winds, endeavour to keep the bow pointing into the wind whenever possible; the streamlining of the boat will part the wind rather than block it. When moving the boat, tack if necessary rather than allow the wind and waves to batter the side of the boat causing it to roll, sometimes severely. It is not only unpleasant to be in a severely rolling boat, which can cause those who are not good sailors to feel queasy, but it is also unsafe.

The chances of falling in can be minimized by remaining seated at all times. If it is necessary to stand up, keep as low as possible and stand astride the boat seat. If the boat rocks and you begin to lose balance it is simply a matter of sitting down. Stability is all about keeping the centre of gravity as low as possible. Fishing whilst seated is not only safer, it also presents a lower profile to the fish, and as a consequence the chances of alarming them are much reduced. Why so many anglers stand to cast and fish, which causes the boat to rock, rather than do it sitting comfortably and hidden from the trout is something that is not easy to understand, but many do.

When lowering anchors over the side do it slowly, letting out the rope hand over hand, making sure that the ropes are not entwined around feet or legs. It has not been unknown for an angler to throw the anchor over the side and promptly follow it as a result! It sounds funny, but it can have disastrous consequences. Doing the job slowly and carefully is not only safer but also less likely to disturb the fish.

It is usual to drop the anchor (or drogue) from the right side of the boat (looking forward) and fish from the left-hand side (if the angler is right handed) so that the flies are not cast over the motor where they could catch and become entangled.

Keeping Out of Sight of the Fish

Once trout catch sight of the angler they become wary, and it is therefore prudent to take every possible step to ensure that they

Craig Barr holds a stunning silver Rutland rainbow. Look at that tail! (Photo courtesy of Anglian Water Hooked *magazine – Cliff Waters.)*

are unaware of your presence. Due to the reflective and refractive properties of water, the fish are only able to see out of it through what is described as a 'window', which takes the form of an 83-degree cone radiating from the trout's eye to the surface; the rest of the water surface outside this window acts as a mirror through which the fish cannot see and which presents a reflected image of the bed of the reservoir. Flies in the window will be silhouetted against the sky, whereas those outside it will be seen against a reflection of the bottom.

As a result of the refraction of light, there is a blind area inside an angle of 10 degrees above the water in which virtually nothing is visible to the trout. Keeping a low profile so that the angler's silhouette is kept within this segment will ensure that his outline is invisible to the fish. It follows that, in order to keep out of sight, a standing angler must of necessity fish at a greater distance and cast a longer line (in the order of 4yd further) than a seated one.

The table opposite shows the relationship between the depth of the trout, the size of the window, the height of the angler's profile, and what the trout can see. The figures clearly demonstrate that keeping low (by remaining seated) pays dividends.

Anchored Boat

Fishing from a boat that is anchored gives the flexibility of fishing anywhere on the water providing it is allowed in the fishery rules (sometimes wildlife reserves, areas around draw off and aerator pipes, and the courses used for yacht races are excluded). It also provides a stable position from which to fish nymphs and deceivers slowly and delicately. Retrieving a team of flies from such a position is simple and effective, and it can be done with great precision if the conditions are right, which is not always as often as one would wish. In typical British weather a strong wind may be swinging the boat around unnaturally. Under such circumstances maintaining the rod in a stable position is difficult. The movement of the boat causes the flies to be dragged unnaturally as it goes one way and then slack line is given to the flies as the boat goes in the opposite direction.

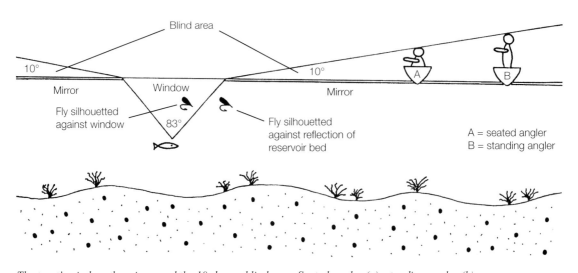

The trout's window, the mirror and the 10-degree blind area. Seated angler (a), standing angler (b).

Closest distances at which the angler will remain hidden from the trout due to the refraction of light

Depth of fish (ft)	Diameter of trout's window (ft)	Minimum distance (yd) at which a seated boat angler and a wading angler (both 4ft high) will remain hidden	Minimum distance (yd) at which a standing boat angler (6ft high) will remain hidden
2	3.5	8	12
4	7	9	13
8	14	10	14
12	21	11	15

Anchoring from the side provides the easiest fishing position, as the angler does not have to cast over the length of the boat; however, when the wind strengthens, attaching the anchor rope from the stern, or in very adverse weather to the bows, cuts down the possibility of the anchor dragging and the boat rolling. Under these conditions, yawing (the tendency for the boat to swing from side to side with the anchor acting as the pivot) will be more pronounced.

To counteract the problem of a dragging anchor let out more rope so that the prongs bite more deeply into the reservoir bed. This may cause the boat to yaw even more severely if only one anchor is used, but at least it will remain where it is wanted. The only way to eliminate yawing altogether is to use two anchors dropped several yards apart, the ropes of which are attached to opposite ends of the boat. Whilst it is very effective and makes for a stable fishing platform, it does entail carrying yet more heavy tackle and it is a cumbersome procedure for a lone angler to perform.

The procedure for mooring using two anchors is as follows. Motor the boat 15yd above and parallel with the intended anchor position and cut the engine. The stern angler drops his anchor 'A' and pays out rope that is attached to the stern of the boat on the starboard (right-hand side looking forward) corner. As the boat continues under its own momentum, 10 or 15yd later the bow angler drops his anchor 'B' over the starboard side and pays out rope that is attached to the bow. The ropes are drawn up until the length of each is approximately equal and the boat drifts down to the fishing position 'C'.

In many ways, when the conditions are perfect, fishing at anchor can be the most leisurely of all methods of fishing, and it is the one that the author chooses first, all other considerations being equal. It can also be the most productive method, as the angler has better control of his tackle. When fishing from a drifting boat, with the

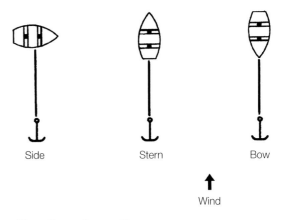

Side   Stern   Bow

↑
Wind

Alternative anchor positions.

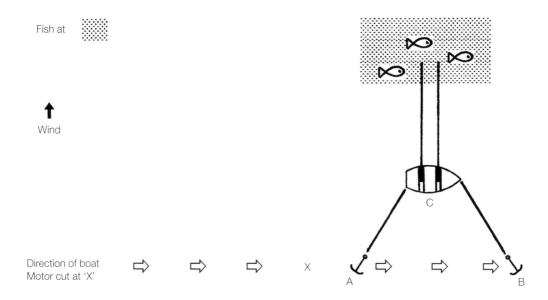

Fish at

Wind

Direction of boat
Motor cut at 'X'

Use of two anchors to counteract yawing.

craft continually catching up with the flies as the drift progresses, things can never be quite so precise and delicate, and the flies cannot be fished so deep as when everything is stationary and stable.

To sit in an anchored boat, in a comfortable swivel boat seat, in fine weather, with co-operative fish, with none of life's problems on one's mind, and at peace with God and the world... But to get back to fishing.

Drifting Boat: Loch Style

There are two primary loch-style methods used whilst drifting: short lining and long lining.

When short lining, a single false cast is made and the flies are laid on the water a short distance in front of the angler. As the boat catches up with the flies, line is retrieved by drawing it back with the arm whilst simultaneously raising the rod until the bob fly dibbles in the surface. The line is lifted off and the procedure repeated. There is generally insufficient time for the flies to

sink very deep, but when the fish are feeding near the surface it can be a straightforward, leisurely and successful method, and vast swathes of water can be covered, the boat drifting from one side of the reservoir to the other. As each cast is quite short it is unlikely that the fly line will land on top of a fish, which will be spooked and swim off in alarm and disturb others. It is a light line method, and if a lot of short lining is envisaged it might be desirable to purchase an outfit, comprising a 10 or 10½ft rod matched with a no. 5 or no. 6 double taper line, solely for this kind of fishing.

When long lining, a much greater distance is cast each time, with more than one false cast being necessary to extend the line, which lands twenty or more yards away from the angler. Once the flies have landed, they are allowed to sink to the desired depth. Line is retrieved until the flies approach the boat. The rod is then raised and the bob fly dibbled in the surface as in short lining. Once again the procedure is repeated as the boat drifts from shore to shore until

Fishing on the drift at Pitsford Water. (Photo courtesy of Anglian Water Hooked *magazine – Cliff Waters.)*

the fish are found. Much greater depths of water, which are out of range when short lining, can be explored by employing different densities of intermediate and sinking fly lines. When the trout are expected to be cruising at depth, it is the method to try first.

Whichever method is used, drifting the boat gives the angler the option of always fishing new territory, with every cast having the chance of finding the fish and a hook up resulting. If the whereabouts of the fish are not known, drifting is the simplest way of covering large areas of water and finding them. Once the fish have been located it is possible to complete the drift and bring the boat round and repeat the same drift over and over again, hopefully taking a fish or two with each one. Alternatively, it is possible to return to the location of the fish and drop anchor and tackle them quietly from a stationary position.

When returning to the starting position once more, it is important to go *round* the

location of the fish, never *over* their heads, as this could well send them down or scatter them to another location altogether. Fish can be scared very easily, so avoiding noise and vibration is all part of the necessary watercraft. Being organized and not dropping tackle and anchor chains in the boat (or over the side) is a simple precaution to take, but it is fundamental to success.

Drogues

A drogue is a necessity for slowing down the drift of the boat in all but the lightest of breezes, and the position of attachment will determine the way the boat progresses.

For basic loch-style fishing, attachment of the drogue will be from the side; both anglers (if there are two in the boat) will fish straight downwind from the other side on parallel lines. The area each angler can fish is quite restricted, as for safety reasons it is not possible to cast over the other angler's face and head and place the flies elsewhere.

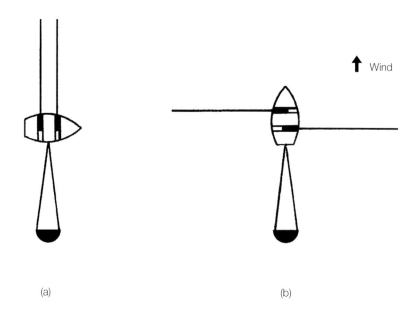

Alternative drogue attachment positions. (a) Side (loch style). (b) Stern (Northampton style).

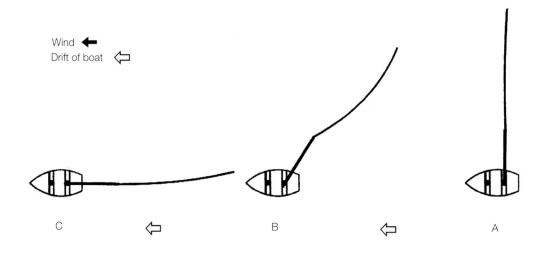

'Northampton' style: line swings behind as boat drifts downwind from 'A' to 'C'. (Drogue omitted for clarity.)

This is one drawback to the approach and vast tracts of potentially productive water cannot be explored.

Drifting Boat: Other Methods

Attaching the drogue to the stern enables anglers to cast to different sides and cover a much larger area of water as the flies swing round and eventually finish up behind the boat as it progresses. These methods are commonly called the 'Northampton' styles of fishing, of which there are several variations.

These methods enable the various depths to be searched more thoroughly to establish the all-important taking level. Continual experimentation is the key until the way that the trout want the flies on the day is discovered (every day will usually be different). The fish will often follow the flies as they are pulled through the water for some considerable time without taking, frequently gently plucking at them. When this occurs do nothing and wait for a positive take,

when the fish will often hook themselves. The trout are often persuaded to seize the flies once they start to accelerate as they begin to swing behind the boat. Employing strong leaders when fishing 'Northampton' style is recommended.

These techniques are used to fish lures, sparkler tubes and large nymphs anywhere from subsurface to very deep, permuting all the variations of line density, the distance cast, the length of line paid out, the angle the line is cast to the boat, the speed of retrieve and the speed of the drift. Performed thoughtfully there is far more skill to the techniques than might at first sight appear – it is much more than simply waiting for a fish to have a go. Although perhaps not fly fishing in the traditional sense of the word, it can sometimes be the only way of tempting a fish on otherwise fruitless days. Regrettably, such times may be accompanied by very light winds, or even a dead calm, and there is simply not enough breeze to propel the boat at sufficient speed, and fishing boats do not have sails!

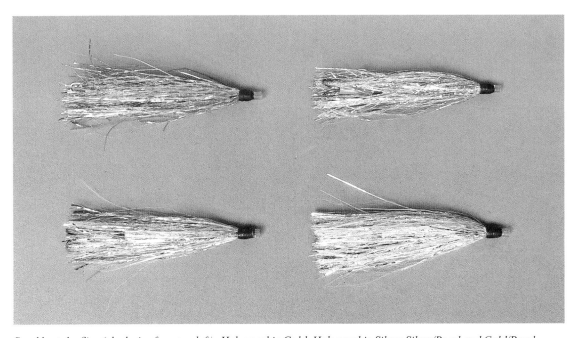

Sparkler tube flies (clockwise from top left): Holographic Gold, Holographic Silver, Silver/Pearl and Gold/Pearl.

Trailing

Allowing the wind to carry the boat and then 'back-drifting' the flies behind it, using an ultra fast sinking line in conjunction with a booby or other buoyant fly, is a way of getting the flies down to the bottom during very warm water temperatures when the fish may be sulking on the reservoir bed and do not really want to know. The method involves casting the flies behind the boat and paying out sufficient line and backing to ensure that the flies reach the bottom and then, as the boat progresses, recovering line until the fish are eventually found.

Disabled and elderly anglers may find that trailing their flies from the back of a drifting boat is the only way they can fish if their incapacity is severe or if casting is painful. It can also be a way of introducing young children, who have not mastered the art of fly casting, to trout fishing. On occasion, trailing can be very successful, but there is little variety in the method and hence many fit and able anglers may well prefer to use other techniques.

Some waters have restrictions on the methods permitted, so it is wise to check the fishery rules. Trolling under motor power is not allowed on reservoirs.

These are the basic drifting techniques, and once they have been practised and mastered it is possible to modify and expand them and move on to other more advanced methods as conditions, experience and the fish dictate. Advanced techniques and disciplines such as rudder fishing, lead lining and float tubing are beyond the compass of this book and so will not be dealt with here.

Float tubing on Thornton Reservoir.

13 Fly Dressing: Good Reasons for Tying Your Own Flies

There must come a point in every fly angler's career when they consider whether or not they should start to tie their own flies. There are many reasons for doing so – cost, durability, quality, the need to modify existing patterns to satisfy local needs, the creation of new patterns, and of course the ultimate satisfaction of catching a trout on something that has been dressed by the angler himself. All these are valid reasons, which will be considered in turn.

Most potential fly dressers will have been put off initially by the thought that their fingers are not dexterous enough, or that their eyesight is not acute enough to produce anything that will deceive a trout. With a little practice, the help of modern tools and vices, and the employment of a good magnifying lamp, it is surprising what is possible and how well the flies turn out.

None of us seem to have enough time and finding more to dress our own flies may seem an impossible luxury for many. Nevertheless, we all manage to find time to do what we really want to do, and once it is discovered that home-produced flies catch far more fish, time will be found to tie them. Fortunately, it is a pastime that can be done at short notice when there is the odd half hour to spare.

The first few attempts may end up being a complete disaster, but practising and mastering the basic techniques that are required will enable acceptable flies to be produced in a very short while. We are indeed fortunate that many of the most successful reservoir flies in use today, such as hare's ear nymphs, pheasant tails, buzzer pupae and tadpoles, to give a few examples, are all very easy to dress and they use inexpensive materials. It is a good idea for beginners to practise and perfect their techniques on such flies before they embark on the more difficult patterns such as clipped deer hair, winged wet and dry flies, detached bodies, and those that employ expensive materials.

It is important to bear in mind that even these early attempts will catch at least as many fish as their shop-bought counterparts, and probably many more.

Cost of Flies

When it comes to cost, unless the angler uses only a limited range of patterns, there will probably be no financial advantage to be gained. The initial outlay on materials, tools and a decent vice can be considerable and could well outstrip any savings in the flies themselves, at least in the early stages. Eventually, the stage will be reached where hooks are the only items to be bought in any quantity.

As in all other areas of fly fishing, it does pay to buy good-quality materials and equipment because anything less will only cause frustration and lead to disappointment. Trying to tie a fly on a hook that slips

The fly dressing bench. Many rewarding hours can be spent tying better and more successful flies.

Although they are not cheap, genetic saddle hackles are a joy to use and they make tying palmered flies effortless.

142

in an inferior vice, or struggling to make do with poor-quality thread or feathers, is enough to try the patience of the most placid of us. On the other hand, there is great satisfaction to be had in possessing and using quality equipment, and in this respect fly dressing is no different to other aspects of fly fishing.

Durability and Quality

When it comes to durability, home-dressed flies come out on top every single time. We have all purchased flies where the whip finish comes undone after a very short while and the fly disintegrates beyond repair, the dressing slips along the hook shank, or the very first trout caught causes so much damage that the fly falls to pieces and has to be discarded. Home fly dressers can take the time and trouble to make sure that their flies are tied tightly, and discreet wire ribbings to strengthen them can be incorporated where appropriate.

Performing such basic procedures as laying down an initial bed of touching turns on the hook shank, applying a drop of varnish to the roots of marabou wings and tails to fix them and reduce the chance of the fibres wrapping around the hook point, running the tying thread through the hackle to bind it down thoroughly, and applying varnish all around the whip finish, all individually take only seconds to do, but they result in flies that last and last.

When it comes to the application of the materials on to the hook shank, we have all bought flies where the dressing has been applied so unevenly that the fly swims on the skew when it is being retrieved, in a manner that must surely alarm any trout with a modicum of intelligence. The standard of some of the cheaper, and sometimes not so cheap, shop-bought and mail-order flies that are available nowadays can only be described as shoddy; perhaps not surprising in a society where price seems to be the only criterion by which products are judged. This philosophy does not help us get the maximum number of takes on our fishing trips.

The home fly dresser can always take off and re-apply any bodies, hackles, and especially wings, with which he is not completely satisfied and which do not sit exactly right. In contrast, the commercial tyer, to whom quantity and not quality is the most important thing, must of necessity carry on and ignore such seemingly minor, but ultimately serious blemishes, so that they can get on to tying the next dozen. The difference between spending 10 or 15min on a single fly, as opposed to a mere 60sec or so, is immense. The home fly dresser is fortunate that he can take his time and does not have to rush things.

Flies that Swim Naturally

It is the author's belief that so long as flies are tied evenly they will catch fish. Even if the amateur fly dresser makes them with heads that are perhaps a trifle large, or with a hackle that is somewhat sparse, or for lack of the correct materials does not follow the original pattern exactly, so long as they swim naturally and true in the water that is what matters. Trout often take their food whilst they are swimming at speed, and they are probably more likely to notice and avoid a poorly tied fly that is wobbling unattractively, in a way no natural creature would, whereas they will probably not have the time to spot any slight deviation in either the choice of dressing materials or in tying technique.

Well-tied flies are highly desirable, and some amateurs produce what can only be described as masterpieces. Although we should always endeavour to produce the very best flies that our skills allow, such a high standard is not essential to deceive

Mal Wright of Leicester, skilled angler, accomplished caster and immaculate fly dresser, lands yet another!

the fish into taking them. We are fortunate that we can learn and progress from our mistakes and improve on the design and technique of the flies as we fish with them, something that it is quite impossible to do with a shop-bought product.

Quality Hooks are Vitally Important

The hook that is employed will always be the most important link between angler and fish, and the home fly dresser can ensure that only suitable, needle-sharp and top-quality hooks that have been individually tested for temper are used. The choice of hook for each individual application is vitally important, and home fly dressers will soon begin to form their own ideas and preferences as to what constitutes the ideal hook for each pattern. This must surely build up confidence, that indefinable element that we know is such a vital ingredient to success.

Sadly, it is still true today that many shop-bought flies seem to be designed to catch fishermen and not fish, some being so grossly overdressed that they are only fit to be stuck into a hat or jacket lapel. This is not helpful to anglers who want to fish with them. The home fly dresser is fortunate that he is not bound by such mercenary and ultimately counterproductive constraints, and can tie his flies as sparsely or as heavily as the pattern demands. He can concentrate on dressing flies that will attract the fish!

Modifications to Existing Patterns

When it comes to all the permutations that are possible with a single fly, it is obvious that the range of patterns available from commercial tyers must of necessity be limited. Yet, as anglers progress they will often find it impossible to locate flies that are exactly what are needed. In such circumstances the need to tie flies to suit one's own individual requirements will become ever more desirable.

Even if one were able to find an obliging custom fly tyer these days, it would be impossible to convey all the nuances that one would wish to incorporate into a modification of a fly to them, and yet by doing the job oneself at the fly-tying bench it is a quick and easy matter. As time goes by it is inevitable that fly patterns will be modified and will slowly evolve into better fish catchers. Fishing experience will determine exactly which changes improve the flies and need to be explored further, and which ones do not and therefore need not be pursued.

Creation of New Fly Patterns

The follow-on to this is the creation of new patterns, and here the field is wide open for

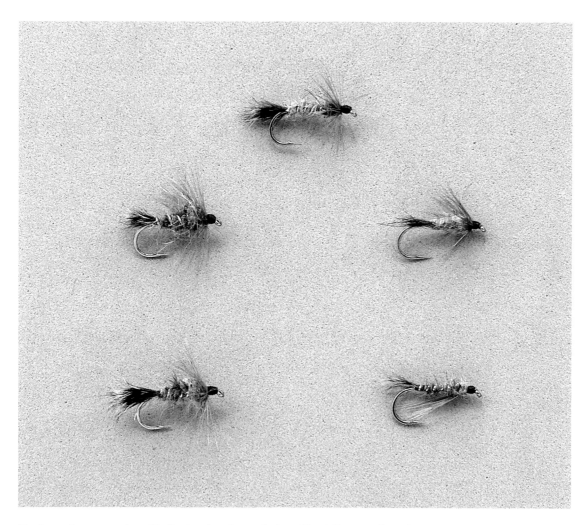

The home fly tyer can dress his flies just how he needs them. Hare's Ear nymphs tied in various styles (clockwise from top): standard, 'low water', skinny, heavily dressed and bushy.

experimentation, especially as new materials come on to the market.

As time goes by it will be inevitable that the thinking angler will come up with new ideas, and the only way to prove them is to tie the flies and try them out for himself. Some of these creations will be successful and others less so, but the experiences gained will all go towards making us better all-round anglers.

King Solomon observed that there is nothing new under the sun almost 3,000 years ago, and all fly tyers will inevitably come across the situation where they think they have 'discovered' a new fly or a new tying technique, only to find that they are reinventing something that was done years ago; it may come as a disappointment, but if more fish are caught in the process that is all that matters.

It is interesting to note that virtually all the truly great and innovative fly anglers over the years, those who have pushed back the boundaries of our sport in ways that have benefited us all, have been fly dressers. For them to innovate their new methods has invariably entailed designing new fly patterns to accompany the theories and techniques that they have devised and perfected. Without their fly-dressing skills they would have been severely hampered and could even have been reduced to the ranks of ordinary fly fishermen.

It is important to remember that the ultimate aim of designing new flies is that of catching more fish; one should never lose sight of this objective. Anyone who sees the creation of new fly patterns merely as a means of satisfying their own vanity and achieving some sort of piscatorial immortality by having their name remembered, like Canon Greenwell, Richard Walker or Arthur Cove, is most likely going to be sadly disappointed!

The Ultimate Satisfaction in Fly Fishing

Finally, there can be no greater thrill than to hook and land a fish on a fly of one's own making, and to accomplish this on a creation of one's own design is even more of an achievement.

Dressing one's own flies makes it possible to keep up with the latest developments in fly design literally on a daily basis, whereas commercial patterns, which in the main emanate from African countries, must of necessity lag behind. In contrast, it is a simple matter to produce copies of new and successful flies at home, which one learns about when talking to other anglers or reads about in the angling magazines.

Another of the benefits of fly dressing is that it opens up the way for new friendships to be formed as a result of discussing flies, materials and fly tying, and trying to overcome the problems that continually arise to challenge the thinking fly fisher.

It can be fascinating to go back and reproduce some of the old and neglected but nevertheless killing flies of yesteryear. It is sometimes surprising to discover how successful some of these forgotten flies can be.

Another bonus of tying your own flies is that it is possible to find a natural fly on your own particular water one day, and then take an artificial that you have devised and tied to imitate it with you on your next fishing expedition.

From time to time the home fly dresser will embark on a new project to copy naturals for which, to his mind, there are no suitable artificials around. To give an example, as has already been discussed, trout do ingest large quantities of buzzer shucks, and it is the author's current project to try and produce a killing pattern that more accurately imitates them. Exactly how the form and translucency of the natural shuck can

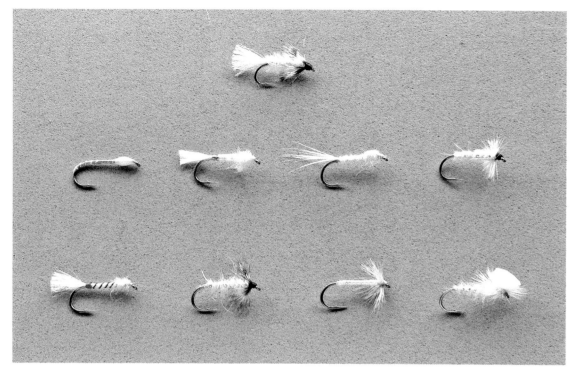

The author's recent attempts to produce a better shuck pattern. Current version (top) and experimental versions below.

be copied with the materials available at the present time, and still fish in the surface film, is open to conjecture, but nevertheless experiments such as this do go on regularly at a thousand fly-dressing benches.

There will always be the blind alleys that we all go down in our quest for ever more successful fly patterns, but these can make our achievements, when they come, all the more sweet. It is amazing how many of these new flies, whilst not being the deadly ones we had hoped for, nevertheless still take their fair share of fish.

An Encouragement to Start Now

After discussing the fishing benefits of tying your own flies, there is one other benefit that ought to be mentioned that has little to do with fishing, which is that fly dressing is a relaxing, peaceful and even therapeutic pastime in its own right. Indeed, there are even a few folk who do not fish at all but simply tie flies for the sheer pleasure of it. That being the case, when the cares and pressures of the world start to get on top of us and burden us down, what better way of relieving the stress can there be than to spend half an hour or so at the fly-tying bench quietly tying a few favourite flies? It can almost be guaranteed to help us unwind and relax.

The benefits of tying your own flies are numerous. The rewards in terms of more pleasure, more fish and a more fascinating sport will most certainly make it well worthwhile. Once you have caught trout on flies that you have designed and tied yourself you will never go back to shop-bought patterns. That is a promise!

14 Recommended Fly Patterns

Every trout fishing book inevitably includes a list of recommended fly patterns, and this one is no different. The ones that follow have caught their fair share of fish; that has been the sole criterion for their inclusion. Many of the dressings are not new. Some are exactly as per the originals, others are but slight variations of old and well-known patterns, and a few are of my own design. Nevertheless, they have all proved their worth over recent seasons. There is no reason to stick slavishly to established fly dressings. If we can improve catch rates by making modifications to existing patterns for our own particular needs and the waters fished, so much the better.

In most of the flies recommended in this chapter there is at least one definite point of concentration such as a bright tag, prominent cheeks, or a recognizable bold (but not huge) varnished black head. I believe that when we observe something we will unconsciously pick out a feature as both a recognition and a focus point. If we were looking at a person it would be the eyes or the mouth, if looking at a motor car perhaps the radiator grille or the badge. In the same way it is likely that the trout, rather than observing the general form, will pick out a particular point of interest and recognition, so I aim to give them one.

Use a fine tying thread. I use Sparton Micro; it is thin and strong and avoids the problem of bulky heads that result when extra turns have been used for whatever reason, and a micro thread seems to grip and hold the materials tighter on the hook shank (which I coat initially with a thin layer of hard wax) so that they do not slip.

Suitable Hooks

I avoid thick wire hooks and those with rank barbs; often when retrieving very slowly, as we generally do with nymphs, a trout is 'on' by just a gentle tighten, and we do not have the chance to lift into the fish (I deliberately avoid the word 'strike'). A finer wire hook has more chance of penetrating the fish's mouth. In these circumstances a fish can be played out and netted quite safely, with little chance of it escaping, providing a tight line is maintained at all times, but the hook drops free immediately the fish is in the net and the pressure on the fly is released.

After a while every fly dresser will begin to form his own opinion about what constitutes a good (and a bad) fly hook, but the following three ranges of Kamasan hooks are excellent designs. They are all forged, which counteracts the tendency for hooks to open out when a fish is being played, they have small barbs that go in easily, and they are made from relatively fine wire, which aids penetration. They are good value for money when bought in bulk, but they are not a 'cheap' hook that will let you down. Starting with these hook patterns will enable most types of fly to be tied, and the fly dresser can add other designs later if it is felt to be necessary.

Selection of Kamasan fly hooks

Pattern	Features	Uses
B400*	Forged, round bend	General hook for nymphs and wet flies.
B405	Forged, short shank	For dry flies and wet flies. Also useful for patterns with bulky bodies: the wide gape avoids the hook point being masked.
B800	Forged, long shank	A strong lure hook.

*If extra large fish are anticipated the heavier B175 could be substituted.

The dressings that follow are described in quite precise terms, as sometimes those we come across are not very explicit; for example, is the hackle a beard or a collar hackle? Is the body tied slim or bulky? These things do matter if we want an exact reproduction and that is why such detail is included here.

The number of flies in this section has been cut down to a reasonably manageable quantity, and although there are twenty-three basic patterns (plus a few terrestrials that will be needed only rarely, and some lures) there should be sufficient upon which to build a sound and versatile angling philosophy. The reader will no doubt wish to supplement them with some of his own patterns (a few more suggestions are included in Appendix I). The author's fly boxes are augmented by (or should it be cluttered up by?) other patterns that are there 'just in case', although it is probably true to say that if the following patterns do not work when used at the appropriate time and in the appropriate way, other patterns most likely won't succeed either.

It is interesting to note that as experience is gained and catch rates increase, so the number of patterns employed seems to decrease proportionately, and it is likely that over the years one or two of the flies may eventually drop out of the list. If I was forced to choose a handful of patterns and fish only with those, I would probably go for the Tadpoles, Dawson's Olive, Holographic Buzzers, Gold Ribbed Hare's Ear, Olive Grizzle Palmer and Booby and would be quite content with those six flies (and their variants) in most circumstances likely to be encountered.

Although the current fashion seems to be to give new flies fancy (and sometimes outrageous) names, the ones of my own design, and those of existing patterns that have been modified, are called by what best describes them. This suits me and enables quick identification of the fly in my box from my fishing records. The flies have deliberately not been divided up into attractors, nymphs or lures, and so on, as many of these flies can move from one category to another as the method of fishing and the corresponding retrieve rates vary.

Subsurface Patterns

BLACK & GREEN TADPOLE
and variants

Hook	Kamasan B800 long shank sizes 8 to 12, weighted if required, and B400 sizes 10 and 12
Tying thread	Black

Tail	Black marabou, with two strands of silver holographic tinsel tied in either side (optional)
Body	Rear: Three turns of fluorescent lime-green chenille; front: black chenille. Use wool instead of chenille for the B400 versions
Hackle	Collar hackle of black cock
Head	Black thread varnished

Variants: Olive Tadpole: substitute olive marabou for tail, olive chenille for front of body and olive-dyed hackle. White Tadpole: substitute white marabou for tail, white chenille for front of body and white hackle. Orange Tadpole: substitute fluorescent orange chenille for rear of body and an orange-dyed hackle. As a further variant an orange marabou tail can be substituted.

So that I can recognize weighted flies at a glance in my fly boxes, I put a tiny dab of red varnish on top of the fly head of all my leaded patterns. This and the following three flies can be tied as goldheads.

BLACK & GREEN MARABOU

Hook	Kamasan B800 long shank sizes 8 to 12, weighted if required
Tying thread	Black
Tail	Black marabou
Body	Rear: three turns of fluorescent lime-green chenille; front: black chenille, ribbed with medium oval silver tinsel (optional)
Hackle	Collar hackle of black cock
Wing	Black marabou
Head	Black thread varnished

This is a simple variation of the Tadpole with a marabou wing added to give it more life and movement.

CAT'S WHISKER

Hook	Kamasan B800 long shank sizes 8 to 12, weighted if required
Tying thread	Black
Tail	White marabou, with two strands of silver holographic tinsel tied in either side (optional)
Body	Fluorescent lime-green chenille
Wing	White marabou
Head	Two bead chain eyes tied with a figure of eight under the hook shank

This is probably the most popular and versatile fly of all time and it can be used as a lure, a deceiver, a general attractor, a highly visible fly in coloured water or as a fry pattern. It can also be tied as a 'mini lure' on B405 hooks sizes 10 and 12.

DAWSON'S OLIVE

Hook	Kamasan B800 long shank or B405 sizes 8 to 12, weighted if required
Tying thread	Black
Tail	Golden olive marabou
Body	Olive chenille, ribbed with medium oval silver tinsel
Hackle	Yellow-dyed guinea fowl tied as a beard hackle
Wing	Olive marabou
Head	Bold head of black thread varnished

Orange variant: substitute orange marabou for the tail and orange guinea fowl for the hackle.

Recommended flies I. From left to right: first row: Black & Green Tadpole, Black & Green Marabou; second row: Cat's Whisker, Dawson's Olive; third row: Olive Damsel, Orange Fritz Booby; bottom row: Flexi Bloodworm, GRHE Green Marabou.

This is a 'nymphy thingy' rather than a lure. It can mean anything in the way of food to the fish and is generally fished quite slowly when it will be taken confidently. It is my most successful point fly, and was originally tied as an imitation of a leech.

OLIVE DAMSEL

Hook	Kamasan B400 sizes 10 and 12
Tying thread	Black
Tail	Olive marabou
Body	Olive seal's fur, ribbed with fine oval gold tinsel over body and shellback
Shellback	Pearl film or pearl tinsel stretched over top of body (optional)
Thorax	Olive seal's fur
Hackle	Collar hackle of olive-dyed partridge
Head	Black thread varnished

Variant: Golden olive marabou tail

There are literally dozens of damsel patterns and this one works as well as any.

ORANGE FRITZ BOOBY

Hook	Kamasan B405 size 8
Tying thread	Black
Tail	Fluorescent orange marabou
Body	Orange Fritz
Booby eyes	Two expanded polystyrene beads in stocking net or alternatively use plastazote booby cord. If using polystyrene for the booby eyes, a water-based dope will be necessary to finish off the fly

Variants: Yellow: yellow tail and yellow Fritz body. White: white tail and white Fritz body. Cat's Whisker: white tail and lime-green Fritz body. Viva: black tail and black/green Fritz body

FLEXI BLOODWORM

Hook	Kamasan B405 sizes 8 and 10, weighted if required
Tying thread	Red
Tail	Two 2in strands of red Flexifloss tied splayed apart
Body	Red Glo-brite floss shade 5, ribbed with fine oval gold tinsel and coated with two coats of Hard as Nails varnish
Head	Two 2in strands of red Flexifloss tied forward over eye and splayed apart.

Whether this is actually taken for a bloodworm is not certain, but with a twitched retrieve it can be deadly on the right occasion. Very often the fish will continually pluck, pluck, pluck! Do not strike, but wait for a firm pull and the fish will be on.

GRHE GREEN MARABOU

Hook	Kamasan B400 sizes 10 and 12
Tying thread	Black
Tail	Fluorescent lime-green floss
Body	Fibres of hare's fur tied scruffy, ribbed with fine oval gold tinsel
Thorax	Hare's fur dubbed a little more thickly

Hackle	Collar hackle of honey cock
Wing	Two tufts of olive marabou, each tied at 90 degrees to the hook shank to give width
Head	Black thread varnished

This is generally used as a bob fly, either when palmered flies are not seen to be working or simply for a change. It seems to work best when fished slowly or very slowly. It could simply be taken for a piece of weed.

BLACK & RED HOLOGRAPHIC BUZZER
and variants

Hook	Kamasan B400 sizes 10 to 14 and Kamasan B405 size 8
Tying thread	Black
Body	Black tying thread tied part way round the bend, ribbed with red holographic tinsel
Thorax	Black thread with two cheeks painted on with orange Tulip paint
Head	Black thread

The whole fly is given four coats of Hard as Nails varnish. Two coats are applied before and two coats after the cheeks have been painted on. In crystal-clear water or very bright conditions the orange cheeks can be omitted.

Variants: for alternative colours use holographic green, holographic silver or holographic gold tinsel, all other details remain the same. For a red variant substitute red tying thread, all other details remain the same. Size 8 can be tied with lead under the thorax for those times when it is necessary to fish very deep.

This pattern is my first choice for a buzzer imitation and these days I tend to use very little else because it is so successful. It is simple to tie, although waiting for the coats of varnish to dry is a pain. I allow each coat to dry overnight before the next one. The original probably accounts for more fish than all the variants added together, although to be fair it is on the leader more often.

I used to use curved hooks for buzzer pupae, but they were not quite strong enough in the wire; after a few opened up I switched to B400s, which cured the problem. They do not have the same curve, but the fish don't seem to mind. This fly has been responsible for more than its fair share of large fish.

ROUGH GOLD RIBBED HARE'S EAR (GRHE)

Hook	Kamasan B400 sizes 10 to 16
Tying thread	Black
Tail	Fibres of hare's fur
Body	Fibres of hare's fur tied scruffy, ribbed with fine oval gold tinsel
Thorax	Hare's fur dubbed a little more thickly
Hackle	Collar hackle of honey cock
Head	Black thread varnished

There are probably more variants of this fly than any other, and most of them seem to work at some time or other. The above tying is so successful that I can think of no way of improving on it; apart from the two distinctly different variants listed. If you wonder why such a drab and nondescript fly as this is so successful, put it before a trout and see what it thinks of it!

YELLOW TAG GRHE

As above, but with an attractor tail of yellow Glo-brite floss shade 10, or amber Glo-Brite floss shade 8, cut short.

PHEASANT TAIL NYMPH (PTN)

Hook	Kamasan B400 sizes 10 to 16
Tying thread	Black
Tail	Natural cock pheasant centre tail fibres
Body	Natural cock pheasant centre tail fibres, ribbed with fine copper wire
Thorax	Brown seal's fur
Wing cases	Natural cock pheasant centre tail fibres
Hackle	Collar hackle of dark brown cock
Head	Black thread varnished

Variant: pearl tinsel can be used for the thorax to give a 'Pearly PTN'.

This is another classic nymph. The colour of the pheasant tail fibres, seal's fur and hackle can be varied to give black, red, orange, olive, claret and other colour variants.

FLUORESCENT YELLOW NYMPH

Hook	Kamasan B400 sizes 10 and 12
Tying thread	Black
Tail	Eight strands of Glo-brite yellow floss shade 10, cut ¼in long
Body	Fluorescent yellow chenille
Hackle	Cock dyed fluorescent yellow tied as a collar hackle
Head	Black thread varnished

This fly was designed for one particular fishing condition – when the water is very deeply coloured after heavy rain or by an algal bloom. It is meant to stand out and be seen at those times when the visibility is so poor that the trout can barely see the flies through the murk.

SHUCK FLY

Hook	Kamasan B400 sizes 10 and 12
Tying thread	Black
Tail	White Glo-brite Multi-yarn shade 16, cut ¼in long
Body	White ostrich herl, ribbed with fine silver or gold tinsel
Thorax	White ostrich herl
Hackle	Collar hackle of badger cock
Head	Black thread varnished

Like many successful flies, this one is easily constructed. It is for use when the trout are on the top and mopping up buzzers and shucks in the surface film. It has proved its worth when fished wet as a middle dropper fly, sometimes with a dry fly on the point.

PARTRIDGE & HOLOGRAPHIC SILVER NYMPH

Hook	Kamasan B400 sizes 10 to 14
Tying thread	Black
Tail	Eight strands of holographic silver tinsel, cut ¼in long

Recommended flies II. From left to right: first row: Black & Red Holographic Buzzer, Rough GRHE, Yellow Tag GRHE, Pheasant Tail Nymph; second row: Fluorescent Yellow Nymph, Shuck Fly, Partridge & Holographic Silver Nymph; third row: Grenadier Special, Olive Grizzle Palmer, Red Tag Wingless Wickham's, Zulu; bottom row: CDC Shuttlecock Buzzer, G&H Sedge, Claret Hopper, Seal's Fur Emerger.

Body	Tapered body of holographic silver tinsel, ribbed with fine silver wire
Hackle	Collar hackle of grey partridge
Head	Black thread varnished

When used as a bob or top dropper fly, this fly seems to do well in bright conditions. Exactly what it represents I have no idea, but the flash could possibly represent the air in a hatching nymph or perhaps the air bubble of a corixa. I like using soft, speckled game hackles that move in a lifelike way.

GRENADIER SPECIAL

Hook	Kamasan B400 sizes 10 to 14
Tying thread	Black
Tail	Amber Glo-brite floss shade 8, cut short
Body	Orange seal's fur, ribbed with fine gold wire
Shoulder and body hackle	Ginger genetic cock saddle hackle tied palmer
Head	Black thread varnished

An old classic fly with a point of interest added by the bright tail. This one has not been quite as successful in the last couple of seasons as in the past. Whether this is a blip or a trend remains to be seen. When tying palmered flies I use genetic saddle hackles, because it is possible to tie both the body and the shoulder hackle with just one feather; the quality is superb.

OLIVE GRIZZLE PALMER

Hook	Kamasan B400 sizes 10 to 14
Tying thread	Black
Tail	Phosphor yellow Glo-brite Multi-yarn shade 11, cut ¼in long
Body	Medium olive seal's fur, ribbed with fine oval gold tinsel
Shoulder and body hackle	Dyed olive grizzle genetic cock saddle hackle tied palmer
Head	Black thread varnished

A pattern of my own, which works well as a bob fly, a damsel imitation, or as a general pattern that can mean anything the trout want it to. It can be fished dry.

RED TAG WINGLESS WICKHAM'S

Hook	Kamasan B400 sizes 10 to 14
Tying thread	Black
Tail	Red Glo-brite floss shade 5, cut short (optional)
Body	Flat gold tinsel, ribbed with fine oval gold tinsel
Shoulder and body hackle	Ginger genetic cock saddle hackle tied palmer
Head	Black thread varnished

Variant: substitute pearl tinsel for the body.

Another classic fly with an added bright tail. It can be fished as a dry fly.

ZULU
and variants

Hook	Kamasan B400 sizes 12 to 16
Tying thread	Black
Tail	Red Glo-brite floss shade 5, cut short
Body	Black seal's fur, ribbed with fine oval silver tinsel
Shoulder and body hackle	Black genetic cock saddle hackle tied palmer
Head	Black thread varnished

Variants: substitute green, yellow or amber Glo-brite floss for the tail.

A general bob fly; the red tail may be taken as the haemoglobin 'blow' of an emerging buzzer, or on the other hand it may not!

General Prospecting Leaders

It has been stressed throughout this book that the same methods should not be employed over and over again without thinking. However, there are times when we have very little idea of where to begin, especially on a strange water, when nothing is hatching, observation yields very little and we have not caught that all-important first fish to spoon. On such occasions the following permutations of leader set-up have proved to be useful as a starting point, and they can be mixed and matched as required. Once a better idea of which flies to employ is gained as a result of observation, autopsies, experience, what other anglers are catching on, or just plain hunches, they can be modified as necessary.

Dry Flies

The following four 'dry' flies are as good and versatile a set as will be needed on most occasions, apart from those times when the fish are feeding on terrestrials and a more specific pattern is required. They are not dries in the traditional sense, as they settle in the surface film rather than stand on top of it. Once they have been tied they are treated with one drop of Water Shed, which is allowed to cure, and then floatant is applied to the flies before fishing and periodically thereafter.

CDC SHUTTLECOCK BUZZER

Hook	Kamasan B405 sizes 12 and 14, and occasionally size 10
Tying thread	Red
Body	Orange seal's fur, ribbed with fine pearl tinsel or gold wire

General prospecting wet fly leaders

	Leader 1	Leader 2	Leader 3
Bob fly	Grenadier 14	Rough GRHE 14	Olive Grizzle Palmer 14
First dropper	Rough GRHE 12	Damsel 10 or 12	Yellow Tag GRHE 12
Second dropper	Black & Red Holographic Buzzer 12	Black & Red Holographic Buzzer 10 or 12	Black & Green Holographic Buzzer 12
Point fly	Dawson's Olive 10	Black & Green Tadpole 10	Cat's Whisker 10

Thorax	Orange seal's fur tied thicker
Wing	Eight CDC plumes laid back to back in two groups of four with the tips level and tied in 'shuttlecock' style. Do not trim the ends of the CDC plumes
Head	Red thread varnished

Variants: use red, olive, green, ginger, black or other colour seal's fur.

This floats well and can be pulled under and allowed to resurface with a 'plop'.

G&H SEDGE
(variant of the original)

Hook	Kamasan B405 sizes 10 and 12
Tying thread	Black
Body	Spun natural deer hair clipped to give a sedge profile
Hackle	Ginger cock collar hackle, clipped at the bottom flush with the body
Underbody	Orange, green or cream fluorescent wool
Antennae	Two filaments of 2lb BS clear nylon speckled with a black felt-tip pen
Head	Black thread varnished

Variant: for an extra visible pattern use white deer hair, and fluorescent cream or fluorescent white wool for the underbody.

A buoyant pattern that is useful for general dry fly use, or for the 'washing line' and 'suspended nymph' methods.

CLARET HOPPER

Hook	Kamasan B405 sizes 12 and 14
Tying thread	Black
Body	Claret seal's fur, ribbed with medium pearl tinsel
Legs	Three knotted claret-dyed cock pheasant centre tail fibres tied in at each side of the head (six in total) before the hackle is wound
Hackle	Claret-dyed cock wound as a collar hackle, with the fibres below the hook shank trimmed level with the body. For greater buoyancy the hackle can be tied parachute style around a plastazote foam wing post
Head	Black thread varnished

Variants: for olive, ginger, black or orange, substitute the appropriate colour-dyed materials for the body, hackle and legs.

This is the classic (and probably the best) general emerger dry fly pattern. It catches everywhere when the fish are rising to dries.

SEAL'S FUR EMERGER
(parachute)

Hook	Kamasan B405 sizes 12 and 14
Tying thread	White or black
Butt	Fine pearl tinsel tied slightly round the bend of the hook
Body	Claret seal's fur, ribbed with fine pearl tinsel
Hackle	Claret cock wound as a parachute hackle

Wing post ⅛in square cube of red plastazote foam

Head White or black thread varnished

Variants: for yellow, amber, orange, ginger, green, olive, white or black, substitute the relevant colour seal's fur with a suitably coloured hackle. Trim the wing post to length after the hackle has been wound and finish off with several half hitches.

Select the appropriately coloured artificial when the fish are seen to be taking the emerging stage of any natural fly. It is a suitable representation of a hatching midge, sedge or upwinged fly. It could even be taken for a floating snail.

The above set of flies should cope with most situations likely to be encountered, but in order to deal with those rare occasions when the fish are taking land-born insects it is as well to have a few terrestrial patterns in reserve. The following five flies form a compact range for such times, and they are all relatively close copy imitations.

Terrestrial Flies

Once terrestrial flies land on the water they soon become waterlogged and unable to escape. These artificials are designed to sit low in the surface film.

DADDY LONG LEGS

Hook Kamasan B405 size 8

Tying thread Black

Body Detached natural elk or deer hair body, ribbed with black tying thread

Legs Four twice-knotted natural cock pheasant centre tail fibres tied at each side of the head and pointing backwards Richard Walker style (eight in total) before the hackle is wound

Hackle Dark brown cock tied as a collar hackle, clipped at the bottom flush with the body. For greater buoyancy the hackle can be tied parachute style around a plastazote foam wing post

Wing Sparse wing of white polypropylene yarn tied back in a 'V'

Head Black thread varnished

HOVER FLY (OR DRONE FLY)

Hook Kamasan B405 sizes 12 and 14

Tying thread Black

Body Black floss silk, ribbed with yellow floss silk

Hackle Grizzle cock tied as a collar hackle, clipped at the bottom flush with the body

Wing Short wing of white polypropylene yarn tied back in a 'V'

Head Black thread varnished

Recommended flies III (terrestrials). From left to right: top row: Hover Fly, Hawthorn Fly; centre: Daddy Long Legs; bottom row: Flying Ant, Terrestrial Beetle.

HAWTHORN FLY

Hook	Kamasan B405 sizes 12 and 14
Tying thread	Black
Legs	Two strands of peacock herl knotted once and tied in trailing the fly
Body	Bronze peacock herl
Hackle	Black cock tied as a collar hackle, clipped at the bottom flush with the body
Wing	Short wing of clear Raffine tied back in a 'V'
Head	Black thread varnished

Variant: if the rather fragile legs come adrift you now have a black gnat!

FLYING ANT

Hook	Kamasan B405 sizes 12 and 14
Tying thread	Black or brown
Body	Black or brown tying thread thorax and abdomen, with a clearly defined waist in between, coated with Hard as Nails varnish and allowed to dry

Hackle	Black or dark brown cock tied as a collar hackle, clipped at the bottom flush with the body
Wing	Short wing of natural CDC
Head	Black or brown thread varnished

TERRESTRIAL BEETLE

Hook	Kamasan B405 sizes 8 to 14
Tying thread	Black
Body	Black seal's fur tied fat, ribbed with fine silver wire, with the fibres below the hook well picked out with a dubbing needle
Back	Black foam tied in at the tail and brought forward to the head and tied down
Head	Black thread varnished

Natural Flies and Some Suggested Artificials

The table on the following page shows some basic suggestions of what pattern of fly could be offered to the trout when observation or an autopsy has identified what the trout are taking. It must be emphasized that what is listed is merely a basic starting point of reference, and it is up to the angler to use his knowledge and experience to make whatever substitutions he deems to be necessary.

Tables such as this, if followed without any thought, could prove to be unhelpful in the long run. It should certainly not be followed slavishly. The author did have some misgivings about whether to include it, but it is reproduced with that salutary note of caution.

Many of the artificial flies that have been considered previously and are included in the table are 'calculated suggestions' that can mean more than one thing to the trout and several of them are listed in more than one category. Flies such as the hare's ear and pheasant tail nymphs in particular are so successful because they have this general but unspecific appeal to the trout. They can mean to the trout what it is anticipating, or maybe what it is not expecting but finds appealing nonetheless in its search for food. This is an added bonus for those of us who fish with these wide spectrum artificials – we may have incorrectly observed what is happening but we are still fishing a suitable fly in spite of our misjudgement!

Flasher Lures

As the reader will know by now, stripping flashers at high speed is not one of the author's favourite tactics – not because it is not a successful technique, it most certainly is, but rather because the continuous casting, the fast retrieves, and the lures used tend to approach the ethos of spinning rather too closely for his liking. Other methods are closer to traditional fly fishing. It is up to each individual to decide which methods he prefers to use and which ones he would rather avoid – but he should never attempt to force his self-imposed principles on to others.

To ignore lures completely is to needlessly reduce the possibility of consistent bags, because there are occasions when the other methods outlined simply do not work, and when lures are what the trout want they should be employed without any qualms. With that purely personal proviso out of the way, it is recommended that the reader carries a few lure patterns in different sizes and in the most successful colours for use at the appropriate time.

Natural creatures and suggested artificial flies to employ

Natural	Nymph/larva	Pupa	Emerger/adult
Buzzers/Midges	Flexi Bloodworm Red Holographic Buzzer Red PTN	Holographic Buzzer in various colours PTN in various colours Shuck Fly	CDC Shuttlecock Buzzer in various colours Hopper in various colours Seal's Fur Emerger
Daphnia	n/a	n/a	Orange Tag GRHE Peach Baby Doll★ Orange Dawson's Olive GRHE Green Marabou Dawson's Olive
Damsels	Olive Damsel Dawson's Olive Olive Grizzle Palmer	n/a	n/a
Sedges/Caddis	Black Tadpole Stick Fly★ PTN Rough GRHE	Rough GRHE Grenadier Special	G&H Sedge Deer Hair Sedge★ Seal's Fur Emerger
Water bugs	n/a	n/a	Rough GRHE Grenadier Special Olive Grizzle Palmer Partridge & Silver Zulu and variants
Upwinged flies	Olive PTN Rough GRHE Olive Grizzle Palmer	n/a	Olive Hopper Wingless Wickham's★ Greenwell's Glory★
Fish and fry	n/a	n/a	Cat's Whisker White Tadpole Pearly PTN (for pin fry) Floating Fry★
Snails	n/a	n/a	Orange or Ginger CDC Shuttlecock Buzzer Ginger Seal's Fur Emerger
Terrestrials	n/a	n/a	Daddy Long Legs Corresponding dry artificial
Weed	n/a	n/a	GRHE Green Marabou Olive Grizzle Palmer Olive Damsel Dawson's Olive

n/a = Not applicable. ★Generally available patterns; dressings not included here.

Recommended flies IV (flasher lures). From left to right: top row: Black Chenille, Christmas Tree; second row: White Marabou, Appetiser; third row: Whiskey Fly, Mickey Finn; bottom row: Alexandra, Jersey Herd.

163

15 The Weather, Water Conditions and Seasons, and their Influence on the Fish

There is no doubt whatsoever that the prevailing conditions do make a significant difference as to whether the trout will be on the feed or not, and consequently whether or not they will be in a mood to take artificial flies. Nevertheless, anglers do blame the conditions for lack of success, rather than their own deficiencies, perhaps far too often. Knowledge of how the conditions affect the fish will help us understand how they may be behaving, and this will consequently help us catch more of them. Each aspect will be looked at in turn, although it is important to remember that when considering the weather and seasons the words 'always' and 'never' are not well suited to our considerations.

Absolutely perfect conditions do not occur very often, certainly not as often as one would like, but that should not deter us from trying to outwit our quarry during seemingly adverse circumstances. The 'stay at home' angler will not learn very much. It is far more satisfying to winkle a few trout out in unfavourable conditions than during those times when everything is spot on and the fish go crazy. That is all part of the challenge of pitting our wits against a wily and vigilant natural adversary.

Water Temperature

By design, trout are cold-blooded creatures, and their level of activity is largely determined by the temperature of the surrounding water. In their native environment they are a fish that is found and breeds in cold and running water. They are very adaptable however, and although reservoirs are generally alien surroundings, they do thrive in most of them. Most water supply reservoirs do not support a breeding population of fish and rely on artificial stocking, although a few brown trout may migrate up feeder streams to spawn if they are able to do so.

Hot weather and its resultant warmer water temperatures make the trout somewhat languid and lethargic, and they will retire to the colder water in the deeps and become disinclined to feed. Very cold water, on the other hand, slows down their metabolic rate, and any food that they do eat is digested very slowly; as a result they become semi-comatose. At both extremes of the temperature range they are, as a consequence, harder to catch.

The table opposite is an adaptation of a well-known one. It summarizes in very general terms the prospects of the trout feeding at various water temperatures. It is not foolproof, but it is a helpful guide nonetheless.

Carrying and using a thermometer to check the water temperature is well worth the small effort involved.

Air Temperature

The air temperature should make little difference to the trout, because it inhabits a completely different environment altogether. One of the main differences it does make, one would guess, is to the angler! When the weather is good, the temperature reasonable, and all is well with the world, we are in good spirits and fish all the better as a result. When the converse applies our performances consequently suffer. Nevertheless, there is one occasion when the trout do seem to discern what is happening and that is when the air temperature drops very suddenly in late afternoon, often with a mist rising from the water, and at such times they seem to go off the feed almost instantaneously.

It is possible to catch trout both in winter when the temperature is cold and in summer when it is warm. In Britain we do get extremes at either end of the scale, which the trout dislike, but far more infrequently than we would perhaps like to admit.

Prospects of trout feeding at various water temperatures

Water temperature (°C)	Trout feeding prospects
Below 4	Poor
4–6	Fair
8–10	Good
12–16	Very good
18	Good
20	Fair
Above 20	Poor

Constant temperatures, whether warm or cold, do not seem to worry the trout, but rapid changes seem to disturb their feeding pattern.

In the recent past the trout fishing season stretched from around late March until late October and it was considered to be a warm weather sport. The situation has changed radically so that now it is an all year round pastime, with many fisheries never closing. There will be opportunities for the angler to fish at any time. Whether he wants to fish in a February gale in sub-zero temperatures is, of course, another matter.

Weather

A warm and dry day makes fishing pleasurable and our performances reflect this.

When it is raining, using fishing tackle becomes more uncomfortable. Wet hands, wet tackle, wet clothing, wet surroundings, rain down your neck; they all make life more difficult and for whatever reason catch rates do fall. When the rain is torrential and vast amounts of very cold water are being deposited into the lake, it makes a significant difference to the trout and they become very hard to catch.

The one time when we *must* stop fishing is when there is a thunderstorm, due to the risk of being struck by lightning. This is multiplied by the vast and flat open spaces of reservoirs; safety dictates that we should either be in the car or in the lodge bemoaning the weather, not waving a carbon fibre lightning conductor about!

Modern fishing clothes and waterproofs are such that they will keep us warm and reasonably dry in virtually any conditions likely to be encountered in Britain.

Cloud Cover

Cloud cover is important to the fish and therefore is important to the angler. Trout

These gathering storm clouds over Eyebrook Reservoir remind us that the forces of nature have far more power than we sometimes realize.

do not like bright sunshine, especially in summer when the sun is high overhead, as they do not possess eyelids or have an iris in their eyes as humans do. As a consequence they are unable to cut down the amount of light reaching the retina when light levels are high. In bright light they are almost in a state of blindness when they are near the surface, and to avoid this uncomfortable state of affairs they go down the water strata until they reach a level of light that is more acceptable.

Overcast conditions suit the fish more, and they are able to feed in the surface layers in comfort, at a light level that is to their liking, and where their food will probably be hatching. When such conditions exist, and the trout's vision is at its most acute, is the time when the thinking angler should pay extra attention to blending into the surroundings. The five 'Ss' of the commandos are worth remembering: shape, shadow, shine, silhouette and sound. Get those right and the trout are far less likely to detect the presence of the angler.

Wind Direction

Anglers have always had their own folklore about wind direction and the following lines of doggerel (of which there are numerous variations) are probably the most well known:

When the wind's from the East,
the fishes bite least,
When the wind's from the West,
the fishes bite best,
When the wind's from the North
the angler goes not forth,
But a wind from the South
blows the bait in their mouth!

It may sound a bit dated but there is a lot of common sense there nevertheless. North and east winds tend to blow from Scandinavia, bringing with them cold air. Cold air striking the water surface inhibits fly hatches, which in turn inhibits the trout from feeding near the surface. Moreover, the cold air does not make fishing as pleasurable as when the weather is warm. That is not to say that trout cannot be caught with the wind coming from these points of the compass, they most definitely can, but it tends to mean sunken flies and possibly sinking lines are more likely to be the order of the day.

On the other hand, southerly and westerly winds generally bring warmer air from the Gulf Stream, which promotes insect activity and fly hatches. In consequence the trout, which is a hungry predator and almost invariably on the lookout for a meal, will be actively searching for food and hopefully our flies. At such times we should rub our hands in anticipation of a good day out and make the most of it.

Wind Speed

The wind speed does not make a lot of difference to whether the trout will be feeding or not. Somewhat surprisingly, when wind speeds are high they may be feeding close to the surface and not on the bottom as logic might perhaps suggest. Strong winds do make a profound difference to presentation however. When the wind is blowing a gale it is sometimes almost impossible to get the flies on to the water, let alone in a way that is going to fool the fish.

When boat fishing, severe and gusty winds not only make fishing unpleasant and sometimes unsafe, but the rocking of the boat will compound the problems as the rod tip lifts up and down and upsets any attempt at good presentation when trying to fish delicately. In such circumstances pulling a lure with a sinking line may be the only feasible option.

On the more exposed waters, the author considers a 15mph wind strength to be the maximum for pleasurable fishing from the boats. Others can and do go out in much higher wind speeds, and they catch fish too; good luck to them! Generally speaking, when the wind speed is much above Beaufort force 4 and there are white horses out on the lake, I won't be joining them!

Checking the weather forecast before a fishing trip is recommended, and television weather text pages are available throughout the night. If the wind is very strong, boat fishing may well have to be postponed.

Barometric Pressure

The barometric pressure does not appear to influence the trout overmuch, apart from those times when it is very low or it is rising or falling quickly (and to a lesser extent when it is very high). Rapid changes in pressure signify high winds and changes to the weather pattern, and any marked change in the weather upsets the prospects of the trout feeding. Settled periods with a steady barometer suit the fish best.

When the pressure falls rapidly, with black thunderclouds on the horizon, signifying the imminent approach of a thunderstorm, the trout seem to go off the feed quite quickly.

They may not resume feeding again until the storm has passed. Although I have not collected sufficient data to be categorical on the subject, if memory serves me correctly I can recall seeing very few (if any) fish caught by those foolhardy anglers who have stubbornly chosen to remain on the water and continue to fish during a thunderstorm. No trout is ever worth taking the ultimate risk of losing one's life.

Water Clarity

The clarity of the water, or the lack of it, generally makes little difference to whether the trout will feed or not. Only when the water has become very muddied by an input of heavy choking silt or clay in suspension is it likely to put the trout off the feed, and this is more likely to happen with rainbows than browns. Algae blooms and similar natural occurrences seem to make little difference to the trout, and they appear to carry on life as normal. What does change, however, is the ability of the fish to see the flies. If they cannot see them, they cannot take them.

In very coloured water during an algal bloom, when the water can almost take on the appearance of pea soup, the trout will have a very restricted view with visibility perhaps down to less than a foot to human eyes. At such times it is necessary to show them something they can at least see. The Fluorescent Yellow Nymph was designed specifically for times such as these. Leader visibility is of far less importance in coloured water conditions, and using multiple droppers is a necessity to ensure that the fish can see at least one fly. Against all seeming probability, large bags can often be taken at such times.

In very clear conditions trout can see a long way, probably much further than

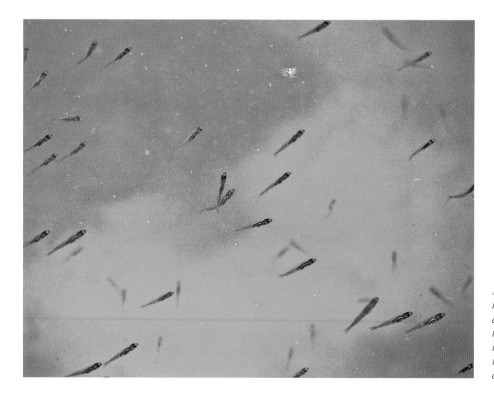

Algae blooms make little difference to the trout. Tiny fry in the margins in deeply coloured water.

would be imagined, and certainly much further than humans can in the same circumstances. We need to get our presentation absolutely right in crystal-clear water, and to use as fine and as long a leader as can be comfortably managed. It may also be necessary to cut down the number of droppers so that the trout do not see more than one fly at a time.

Seasonal Changes

Exactly where in the reservoir the majority of trout are to be found varies according to the time of year, but in *very* general terms can be summarized as follows:

- Early season: the trout will be in the marginal shallows where they will be feeding hard to pack on weight after the winter.
- Early summer: migration to deeper water during the day but often returning to the margins to feed in the evening. If there is a hatch of insects it may bring about a general rise. The trout may remain there until early morning. Food for the fish will be in abundance at this time, but they may not be quite so co-operative with artificial flies because they have so much choice in the way of natural food.
- High summer: the trout will be largely offshore but high in the water feeding on daphnia, buzzers, nymphs and the like. If the water temperature is very high they may be close to the bottom in deep water where the water temperature is cooler, and doing little feeding.
- Back end: the trout return to the shallows, often accompanied by fry feeding, when they will once again be feeding hard to build up body fat to take them through the spawning cycle and the winter months.

A superb overwintered rainbow of 4lb 9oz with a perfect tail. It was yet another large fish taken on a Black & Red Holographic Buzzer. Bonus trout like this will turn up from time to time.

The best months for the reservoir fly fisher are usually expected to be mid March to mid June and then again in September and October. British weather follows roughly the same pattern each year, but it can be delayed or brought forward by a late spring or an early summer. As a result, sometimes what is anticipated to be a profitable month is not so and vice versa.

Time of Day

Trout do not feed continuously throughout the day, and if it were possible to ascertain exactly when they will be feeding we would be able to save a lot of time and catch more fish. Sadly, the fish are extremely unpredictable and the old adage that they feed around the middle of the day early and late in the season, and during the morning and evening in the middle months is, in the author's experience, not very reliable. The weather plays an important part in this, and a change in conditions can quickly upset the anticipated state of things. There are times when the fishing has been slow during the day and nothing has been hatching; we have then waited for the fish to come on in a feeding frenzy during an evening rise, thinking that they surely *must* be hungry and feed sometime, and been disappointed when it has not materialized.

The best advice is to keep one's eyes open for moving fish and try for them when they are seen, but also to persevere when things are quiet. It is possible to pass our flies right under the noses of the trout, and no matter what pattern we fish, and however we fish it, they do not want to know; then later on in the day and for no apparent reason, almost as if a switch had been thrown, they start to take. It is also the case that if they have been feeding heavily in the morning one day it is no guarantee that the same pattern will be repeated the next!

In high summer, fishing very early in the morning can be productive, and it is sometimes possible to catch most of the fish to be taken before the majority of anglers arrive. It does necessitate getting up while the rest of the world is still comfortably in bed, but it can bring its rewards. Late evenings can prove worthwhile, when the trout start to rise and have their supper as the light begins to fail; if the evening is still warm and the wind drops it is often worth postponing packing up and fishing nymphs or dries right on into the darkness.

As noted previously, those occasions when the temperature drops suddenly and a mist starts to rise from the water generally signals that things are likely to prove difficult, and an early start home might be a good idea.

If the fishing is dead slow it is perhaps time to have a break, eat lunch, and have a chat with fishing companions; but it is suggested that we should never get into the habit of idling time away on the bank. It is far better to change tactics and try something different or move to a different fishing location, rather than simply wait for things to get better.

Weed Beds

During the autumn and winter months the weed beds will have died back due to the colder temperatures and the low levels of light. When the fly fishing season re-opens in March there will be little weed growth in the margins and most parts will be completely weed free. As the temperature and the amount of sunlight increases in the spring, the aquatic plants will start to grow rapidly, until in June or July vast areas of shallow water may well be covered, or possibly even choked, by the tangle of growth that will often reach to the surface. The feet of wading anglers may well retard this growth in popular areas for a while, but nature inevitably wins through in the end and, unless weed cutting is performed, large areas may be impossible to fish without constant snagging. Deeper water will remain relatively clear as sunlight, being unable to penetrate into the depths, will not be able to stimulate growth; this is particularly the case if the water tends to be coloured.

There will often be gaps and bays in the weed that can be fished, and whilst they are still open they should be given a try.

Fishing around weed beds may not be easy, but the trout's food (and the trout) will be there.

Many anglers avoid such places, as the fishing may not be easy, and will head elsewhere, but they are disregarding the trout's larder. Such places are the habitat of the food items that the fish will be seeking. A handful of weed placed in a container of water will disclose how much aquatic life is present in such places – nymphs, larvae, bugs, snails, small fish; they will all be there in vast numbers, because such places are stores of the micro-organisms on which they in turn feed. Weed beds are also places of refuge for the trout, as predators such as pike, cormorants, mink and the like cannot easily follow them into the tangle.

As we well know, the trout will probably be where their food is, and rather than dismissing weed beds as an inconvenience, they should be looked on as opportunities to find (and catch) the fish.

Stocking Levels

Stocking levels are obviously an important factor in the quantity of fish to be caught, and getting them right is a vitally important role for every fishery manager. The equation that fishery managers have to get right is for customers to catch sufficient fish to be satisfied, with sufficient challenge for

A sweep of the net at Thornton Reservoir in August disclosed this wide variety of fauna: snails, cased caddis, damsel larvae, corixae, freshwater louse, bloodworm, beetles, an upwinged fly nymph, a leech and even two newts! No wonder the trout pack on weight.

them to enjoy and extend themselves, but without the fishing being either too hard or too easy. If they manage to get that right when the conditions are both good and bad (a nigh impossibility in reality) anglers will return once again to part with their hard-earned cash.

Most anglers probably dream of owning and running their own fishery, where they can fish when they like and stock it with what they want to catch. It sounds idyllic, but in truth it is a hard and sometimes thankless job, and when things go wrong it is probably more of a nightmare than a dream!

If stock levels are too low the trout will not be numerous enough to locate, and they will have far too much natural food available to need to forage sufficiently wide and hard to take artificial flies. With such an abundance of natural food the fish will pack on weight and condition. Simultaneously, the population of coarse fish in the water may well increase to such an extent that the trout will be unable to prune them back to respectable levels and the water will decline

as a trout fishery. On the other hand, if stock levels are too high the fish may well climb over each other to take our flies, but as the food supply is insufficient for the number of fish in the reservoir and what it will sustain, they will eventually lose condition.

None of us want the fishing to be too easy, so that four casts will get us two fish at a time and we reach our limit in less than half an hour. Such fishing would quickly become boring and we would soon give up and go elsewhere after the novelty had worn off. On the other hand, we do not want to flog away all day and have no reward for our efforts, especially when we are doing things correctly and feel we rightfully 'deserve' a brace or two.

Conclusions

We should not be put off because the signs are not favourable; and we should not be disappointed when what we expect to be a good day turns out to be a disappointment. That is surely all part of the glorious

Stocking time at Rutland Water: a consignment of fish stocked directly into the reservoir at Whitwell.

uncertainty of fly fishing! If we knew we would always end up with a bag full of fish the sport would quickly lose its appeal. If I was asked to choose the perfect conditions for fishing I would probably choose a settled warm and dry day in mid May, with a cloudy sky and a southwesterly wind of 10mph – and knowing my luck I would probably blank!

The best advice is to listen to the weather forecast (although they can sometimes be wildly inaccurate), check with the intended fishery to see how it is doing, and then fish it for all it is worth. Few of us are fortunate enough to be able to pick the days when we can fish, and we have to fit fishing in with other things on the calendar; if we waited until everything was absolutely perfect we would probably not do very much fishing! The most satisfying days are often those when the portents are not good but we manage to have a better than anticipated level of success.

16 On the Future of Fly Fishing

For any sport to survive it continually needs new blood coming through to swell its ranks. With fly fishing we seem to be arriving at a watershed: one where older anglers seem to be retiring faster than new recruits are replacing them. Why should this be, and what can be done to put matters right? The reasons for the decline can probably be put down to four main factors: the cost of fly fishing, the safety aspect, the patience and perseverance needed to succeed, and a lack of awareness of our sport by the public at large. Each of these facets will be considered to see what can be done to remedy the situation.

Cost of Tackle

Fly fishing is not a cheap sport upon which to embark, and a set of tackle will be required to make any kind of a start. Good tackle does not come cheap, and most anglers will have found to their cost that whilst the very best and most expensive tackle is not essential, bargain basement rubbish will not be adequate. A set of good basic equipment will be needed to have any chance of success at the outset, and without that initial success many aspiring anglers have sadly given up. Catching trout is the main objective of the exercise, and a modicum of success will spur the novice on to persist and eventually succeed, whereas failure will have the reverse effect. Can we blame any novice for giving up after half a dozen fishless outings?

With the cost of a new fly fishing outfit being somewhere in the region of £150 we are not talking about a trifling sum to outlay on a sport that may not necessarily match up to expectations. We have to be realistic and recognize that not everyone will find fly fishing to their liking, and such a sum is a large one to pay simply to try it out. To youngsters especially, such an amount is a large investment.

Cost of Fishing Permits

The cost of a full-day ticket is not cheap, and thankfully many fisheries now offer special concessions for beginners. One of my 'home' waters, Eyebrook Reservoir, offers a novice permit, which is excellent value for a full day out at a well-kept fishery in beautiful surroundings that is stocked with good-conditioned and hard-fighting fish.

Rod licences are expensive for beginners, and the inducement of a reduced-price novice licence, perhaps for their first season, would probably be an encouragement to beginners. It would also bring in more revenue for the Environment Agency in the long run, once they become regulars. Fly fishing is a sport that, once mastered, is a lifelong hobby, and so they would have customers (and revenue) for life.

Safety of Young Anglers

In days gone by, youngsters would cycle off into the countryside on their own and

With fish like this to be caught we must do what we can to promote fly fishing. Barrie Robinson of Nuneaton with a specimen 6lb 6oz brown trout from Thornton Reservoir.

fish in relatively safe surroundings, but nowadays parents are justifiably reluctant to let their children out of their sight. This means that unless very young anglers are accompanied by a parent or a family friend, they will probably never get the opportunity to experience fly fishing. This is not just a fishing problem, but a result of the kind of society that we live in today, and the dilemma seems to be an insurmountable one in many ways. Regrettably, the negative implications of the Child Protection Act, and the draconian regulations it has brought in, inevitably must, and already has, deterred many folk from helping youngsters they do not know.

On the positive side, fisheries such as Rutland and Grafham offer numerous fly fishing courses run by qualified and vetted professionals; they are an ideal introduction to the sport. From the raw beginner up to the more experienced improver, different courses are arranged to cater for anglers as they progress.

Patience and Perseverance vs Instant Gratification

Unfortunately, in this instant 'just add water' society we live in, the patience and perseverance needed to master the techniques required for fly fishing seem to be lacking in some of today's youngsters. They seem to be blissfully unaware that there can be great satisfaction in slowly mastering and improving the disciplines needed in any sport. This is not isolated to fishing, but to all participation sports; witness the increase in spectator sports and the decline of participation sports nowadays.

The dreaded computer has a lot to answer for, with its seductive promise of bringing the pleasures of every experience into our homes, and the lie that has been perpetrated that it can replace the pleasure and thrill of actually being there and doing things for oneself. In spite of the claims made by computer manufacturers, there can never be any way that a virtual reality computer screen experience by proxy can replace the thrill of doing the real thing. How can you duplicate, by means of a computer display, the real life experience of the sight and feel of the rainbow of myriad crystal water droplets showering from a fish in an icy cascade as it is finally raised in the landing net? It simply cannot be done.

Today there are many youngsters who seem to be proud of the fact that they are 'bored' with everything, and who, rather than learn a new skill or hobby, would rather wander the streets being a nuisance, causing trouble or, even worse, experimenting with drugs or becoming criminals. This is sad for us, but even more sad for them, when they could be doing something constructive with their lives, which would prepare them for living in the real world.

The Mastering of Fishing Skills

Learning to cast a fly is not easy, and it takes a few seasons to be fully proficient, but the emotional reward of being able to master the sheer poetry of casting a fly line is immense. The patience required to persist, sometimes for hour after hour without a pull, is an essential discipline to learn, but it makes the satisfaction of success, when it eventually does come, all the more worthwhile. Surely such skills must prepare us for life and the knocks and bumps that inevitably come along the way.

Joining a fishing club can be a great help for beginners, as they will rub shoulders with, and learn from, other more experienced anglers, and therefore membership cannot be too strongly recommended. I am pleased to record that my own local club, The Leicestershire Fly Fishing Association (www.leicestershireflyfishing.org.uk), wisely has a policy of free membership for juniors.

To be a competent angler involves a wide range of skills – watercraft, casting, some basic entomology, persistence, logical thinking, and even a little good fortune – and they are not acquired instantly. Nothing that is worth anything or worth doing can ever be achieved without determination and application, and learning to catch a trout with an artificial fly is no exception, but the rewards in terms of pleasure and satisfaction are out of all proportion to the effort put in.

Someone who has never experienced the thrill of a trout taking a fly, or felt the adrenaline-pumping experience of playing a lively and powerful trout, or performed the eventual netting of a shimmering rainbow, can have any idea of the emotions that come into play. No wonder that it is us, and not the trout, who *really* become hooked!

Lack of Awareness by the General Public

Considering the vast numbers of anglers who go fishing regularly, fishing in general, and fly fishing in particular, has a very low profile with the general public. One only has to scan the pages of the sports' supplements

The wealth of experience of the Leicestershire Fly Fishing Association – seventeen members who between them have fished for their country forty-two times.

published by the national press to see that we are virtually ignored – when did you last see an in-depth article on fly fishing in the national papers, or detailed fishing reports? There is, of course, the dedicated angling press, which produces a number of fly fishing periodicals that sell in huge numbers, but these never come into the hands of non-anglers.

There have been numerous individual and team successes by British coarse and fly anglers in international events over the years, and, as a nation of anglers, we have a record of which we can be justifiably proud. Nevertheless, in spite of these successes, when has the sports' personality of the year ever been an angler, or when was the last time one was even on the short list? With such poor publicity, is it any wonder that the general public are blissfully unaware of the sport and therefore do not even consider it? One of the problems is that it is not an easy sport for spectators to follow.

It involves long time periods, and the detail cannot be observed at a distance, although much the same could be said about cricket and golf and they have a much greater media profile.

As anglers we may be the butt of jokes, but we do have a fascinating and absorbing pastime that has no equal. More people participate in angling than any other sport, and yet the majority of the general public have no idea of the joys that they are missing!

We Have Good News to Tell

As responsible anglers we have to tell people what a great sport we indulge in and encourage others to have a try if they show an interest. The author recalls the pleasure of taking a youngster down to the local canal one evening recently and teaching him the art of float fishing. The sheer joy of seeing him catch twenty odd tiny skimmers, roach

John Rose of Leicester with a 15lb 13oz rainbow caught on the opening day of the season at Eyebrook Reservoir. It took a small black lure.

Anglers leave the boat dock at the start of a Lexus European Fly Fishing Championship heat at Eyebrook Reservoir. Events like this give much needed publicity to the sport.

and perch for the first time ever in his life was a delight, and although in his innocence the young man thought that it was the fish that were hooked, I knew better! Many such youngsters, once hooked like this, could well be fishermen for life and may eventually graduate to fly fishing.

Giving away a few trout to friends and neighbours is one of the best pieces of propaganda we have and we should employ it whenever possible. A freshly caught reservoir trout beats a sad supermarket one every time, and once people taste the difference they may well become interested in what we do, and how we do it. We all catch far more trout than we can ever eat ourselves, so why not make a point of doing a 'trout run' when the freezer starts to get full.

It is amazing that most non-anglers have simply no idea of what trout fishing is all about. They think that we all spend our days sitting on a basket for hours on end staring at a float that never goes under. Such common misconceptions show that we are not getting the message across. So next time the opportunity arises we must speak up for our sport and tell folk how great fly fishing is, and offer to help them if they want to give it a try. By encouraging more people into the sport, and making them our allies rather than letting them remain uncommitted, is one of the best ways we have of silencing the anti-blood sports brigade who are continually waging a war of attrition against us.

Postscript

What more is there to be said apart from to encourage the reader to keep on striving to improve his performances and catch rates, to keep on experimenting, but above all to keep on enjoying his fishing. Fishing should tax our intelligence – but it should also be fun. Try and remember this on a cold fishless afternoon when the wind is howling and blowing your tackle around, the waves have carried icy cold water over the tops of your waders and it is now trickling down your groin, and your hair is wet because you had to rescue your hat after it had been blown in. Remember that you have come here and spent your hard-earned money on a ticket, not because you will starve if you don't catch a fish, but because you really enjoy fly fishing. Remember that you could have been at home lounging before a welcoming fire, listening to a Beethoven Piano Sonata with a glass of something to cheer you at your elbow. But you, dear angler, would rather be braving the elements, with fingers so cold that they don't seem to belong to you at all, and you are doing this purely for the pleasure of it!

Our Angling Heritage

We should always remember that we are but mere stewards of the great angling heritage that has been handed down to us by our piscatorial forefathers. Like them, we too will one day pass away into obscurity and be forgotten, but what we can leave behind is a sport that is still thriving. That is why we have to help and encourage those who show an interest in our passion as they pass from novice to more experienced angler. If we do not, many of them may well give up due to lack of success and lack of encouragement. A helpful word of advice, and a fly or two passed on from time to time, are surely not too much to give.

The world would be a sadder and more mundane place without such field sports as ours, and we must do all we can to protect and preserve them. Every angler should join the Anglers' Conservation Association (the ACA; www.a-c-a.org) who look after anglers' interests and pursue polluters with unrelenting vigour. Sadly, this group receive little support from the vast majority of anglers. There are estimated to be in the region of two to three million anglers in Great Britain today, and fishing is by far the largest participant sport in this country, but to our shame less than 15,000 of us are actually members of this great organization.

Considering the vast amounts of money that we spend on tackle and fishing, the small annual subscription is a mere pittance. If more of us joined, angling would have a stronger voice and our sport would be more secure.

Good Ambassadors for Fly Fishing

Whether the places we fish are private or open to the general public, we should be

Twelve-year-old Kiri proudly holds her first ever rainbow trout. We must safeguard our sport for youngsters like this.

good ambassadors for our sport by our courteous and polite behaviour.

We should leave no litter, and make sure that we take all our discarded nylon home for safe disposal. We all know the misery that carelessly abandoned fishing line can cause to wildlife, and yet the amount that is still found in the boats and attached to the anchor ropes and elsewhere is staggering. Let us not be guilty of this offence.

We should park our cars with consideration; close farm gates behind us; take care not to break branches, damage hedges or uproot foliage; show consideration for livestock; and when we finally pack up and go home let there be no trace that we have ever been there.

Idyllic Surroundings

I know we are there to fish, but that should not stop us from enjoying either the wildlife or the beautiful surroundings that so often accompany our sport. Those who ignore them are missing so much.

To see a mallard duck proudly swimming and showing off her brood of little ones to the world is a sight to behold, or the heron, like a hunchbacked old man, standing immobile for minutes on end as he waits for his prey to venture within range of his thrusting beak, or the 'V' formations of geese as they come in to land as evening approaches. They resemble squadrons of aeroplanes returning from

Trout fishing often takes place in idyllic surroundings. Normanton Church, built in 1764, is the most famous landmark at Rutland Water.

a sortie, with their deafening 'honking' that makes you instinctively duck beneath them. The sight of swallows, swifts, martins, wagtails, kingfishers, or the song of the skylark on a summer's day as he climbs ever higher singing his praises – it is a wonder that we can concentrate on fishing at all.

There are beautiful sunsets to enjoy as the red evening glow shimmers on the gently rippled surface of the water, the lofty majesty of dark storm clouds that threaten to overcome everything as they approach and remind us that we are merely mortal and puny in the face of such grandeur and power, or the warm sunshine, blue skies and snow-white cirrus clouds.

There are also those times when we are bank fishing all alone on a summer evening and darkness suddenly falls as though someone had turned a dimmer switch; everything goes momentarily quiet and still, with an eerie and supernatural silence. At such times we feel so utterly alone that time seems to stop and have no meaning, and we wonder if we are the only person left in the universe.

Such experiences as these are rightly the inspiration of artists and poets. There are so many wonderful memories that we can take home to recall on cold winter days by the fireside as we reminisce and glory in the greatest of all sports. When we buy our ticket, these things are mere

When the fishing is quiet, why not spend a moment enjoying the beauty of the wildlife? A mallard duck with her young.

bonuses that are thrown in for nothing and we should be thankful and enjoy them to the full.

Fly Fishing has to Move Forward

Whilst it is important that the true ethos and heritage of fly fishing is continued, we must not be carried away by those anglers who would seemingly wish it to remain fixed in time. They conveniently seem to forget the hindrances in the form of inefficient and crude tackle that our predecessors had.

We have all heard those who call for everything new to be banned, whether it be rudders, fishfinders, boobies, or bite indicators. When it comes to banning things, who is the final arbiter, and on what basis are such decisions made? Are they made by those who are jealous and think that every trout caught using these 'new' methods and implements is one less that is available for them to catch? With thousands of trout stocked in reservoirs, there are plenty of fish available to the skilful angler!

We should be pleased when others catch; when they are continually catching and we cannot get a pull, however hard we try, it can sometimes be difficult, but next time it will hopefully be our turn. If it does not affect us or our fishing, let us leave others alone to fish as they wish with the methods they choose and quietly get on with our own without criticism or rancour. We have enough opponents without fighting among ourselves.

We should be thankful and take advantage of everything that new technology has given us. Would we want to be saddled with heavy cane rods, silk lines that need drying and dressing every time, gut leaders that need damping and then still break for no apparent reason, rowing boats that would take half an hour to reach the North Arm, and stocking levels that give a rod average

The end to a perfect day – sunset over Eyebrook Reservoir.

of 0.5 fish per visit as in the 'good old days' gone by? When Eyebrook Reservoir first opened to the general fishing public in 1952 the rod average was 0.46 fish, and it was not until the 1960s that it rose above one fish per rod. Today it ranges between three and four. I for one am more than happy to use light carbon rods, virtually maintenance-free fly lines, man-made tying thread that does not break, tinsel that does not tarnish and hooks with micro barbs. In fact, anything that helps an ordinary mortal to improve his catches just that little bit is more than welcome.

But to end on a more encouraging note, while the trout is there, there will surely be anglers who want to pit their wits against him with a fly. Sometimes we will be successful and sometimes we will fail miserably, but the glorious uncertainty of fly fishing will always draw us back to the water like a magnet. Long may it continue to do so.

Thank you for reading this book. You must surely be an angler of some kind to have waded thus far (no pun intended). May God bless you, and be with you and preserve you, as you engage in what is the greatest sport known to mankind.

Appendix I
Supplementary List of Fly Patterns

All anglers carry far more flies than they will ever need, and more than they will probably ever tie on their leader! The following selection is offered in case the reader wishes to supplement those given in Chapter 14 with a few additional patterns.

Additional patterns. From left to right: first row (nymphs and wet flies): Black & Peacock Spider, Blakestone Buzzer, Cove PTN, Diawl Bach; second row (nymphs and wet flies): Peach Doll, Silver Corixa, Soldier Palmer, Stick Fly; third row (dry flies and emergers): Bibio, Deer Hair Sedge, Shipman's Buzzer, Wickham's Fancy; fourth row (lures): Floating Fry, Minkie; bottom row (lures): Muddler Minnow, Missionary.

Appendix II

Construction Details of Tackle Accessories

Seat Riser

Materials

One piece of wood 7in × 3¾in × 21in (180mm × 95mm × 525mm). You will probably need to glue and screw together two pieces to arrive at the 3¾in thickness. One brass handle and screws.

Construction

Chisel out four recesses 1½in × 1in × ¼in deep (40mm × 25mm × 6mm) to take the webbing at 7½in (190mm) centres; the first two should be approximately 2½in (60mm) from one end.
Varnish to make it weatherproof, and leave to dry.
Screw a brass carrying handle on to the other end.

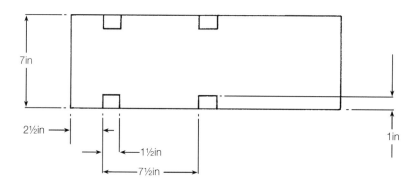

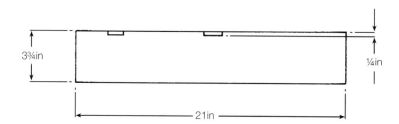

Seat block.

Webbing-to-Clamp Seat Device

Materials

One piece of wood 7in × 11in × 1in (180mm × 280mm × 25mm).
One piece of wood 7in × 6½in × 1½in (180mm × 165mm × 40mm).
Four 50mm no.10 countersunk wood screws.
Four 6mm × 80mm bolts, washers, and nylon insert locking nuts.

Construction

Glue and screw the 7in × 6½in piece of wood centrally on to the larger piece. Drill four 6.5mm diameter holes at $5^5/_{16}$in (135mm) centres through the smaller piece, and counterbore on the 7in × 11in side to take the screw heads below the surface of the wood.

Varnish to make weatherproof and when dry bolt the clamp mechanism on to the 7in × 6½in side.

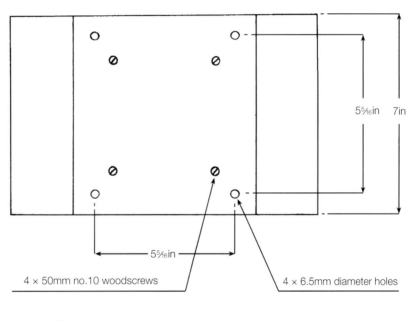

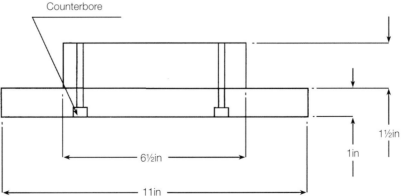

*Webbing-to-clamp
seat device.*

Appendix III
Fishing Record Card

Date:	Day: S M T W T F S	Time fished:	Bank/Boat no:	Mot/Elec/Row

Location:	Air temp: °C	Wind direction:	Beaufort:

Weather:	Water temp: °C	Water colour:

Tackle:	Line density:	Braid:	Leader length: ft	BS: lb

B/R	Place	D/A	Time	Weight	Fly	Hook size	Position	Retrieve	Take	Autopsy
1				lb oz		:				
2				lb oz		:				
3				lb oz		:				
4				lb oz		:				
5				lb oz		:				
6				lb oz		:				
7				lb oz		:				
8				lb oz		:				

Remarks:

Fished with:

Takes: Pulls =

  Hooked & lost =

   Fish =   Unsuccessful methods/flies:

B/R = brown/rainbow; D/A = drift/anchor.

Bibliography

The following books have all proved useful to read more than once, and although some of the information may well have been superseded, the author has no hesitation in recommending them. As with all things it is a good idea to read everything with a degree of discernment.

Angling books come into print, and go out of print again, on a regular basis. A good proportion will not be available from ordinary retail bookshops. There is a large market in second-hand angling books and most can be obtained from specialist angling book dealers.

Clarke, B., *The Pursuit of Stillwater Trout* (A&C Black, 1975)

Cove, A., *My Way with Trout* (Crowood, 1986)

Gathercole, P., *The Handbook of Fly Tying* (Crowood, 1989)

Goddard, J. and Clarke, B., *The Trout and the Fly* (Ernest Benn, 1980)

Ivens, T.C., *Still Water Fly-Fishing* (André Deutsch, 1952)

Mackenzie-Philps, P., *Flycasting Handbook* (Ward Lock, 1991)

Ogbourne, C., *Advanced Stillwater Flyfishing* (David & Charles, 1993)

Pearson, A., *Trout Angler's Angles: An Approach to Stillwaters* (Crowood, 1990)

Saville, T., *Reservoir Trout Fishing with Tom Saville* (H.F. & G. Witherby, 1991)

Walker, C.F., *Lake Flies and their Imitation* (Herbert Jenkins, 1960)

Walker, R., *Dick Walker's Trout Fishing on Rivers and Stillwaters* (Swan Hill Press, 1997)

The following fly fishing and fly casting DVD is highly recommended and should be on every fly angler's shelf for reference.

Evans, M., *Trout Fishing and Fly Casting* (Rapid River)

INDEX

Numbers in italics refer to photographs, fly dressings are shown with an asterisk★.

ACA 180
accessories 27–28, 186–187
AFTM system 34
air temperature 165
algae *168*
anchor 32, 133, 134–136
artificial flies
 Alexandra 61, *163*
 Appetiser *47*, 108, *163*
 Baby Doll 108
 Black & Green Holographic Buzzer 58, *93*, *94*
 Black & Green Marabou *10*, 55, 59, 150★
 Black & Green Tadpole 55, 57, 60, 61, *96*, 149–150★
 Black & Red Holographic Buzzer *frontispiece*, 58, 153★, *169*
 Black & Silver Holographic Buzzer 58
 Black Chenille *163*
 Blakestone Buzzer 55
 Cat's Whisker 57, 59, 61, 125, 150★
 CDC Shuttlecock Buzzer 157–158★
 Christmas Tree *163*
 Claret Hopper 158★
 Daddy Long Legs *20*, 159★
 Dawson's Olive 55, 58, 60, 108, 150–152★
 Flexi Bloodworm 65, 152★
 Floating Fry 125
 Fluorescent Yellow Nymph 154★, 168
 Flying Ant 160–161★
 G & H Sedge 104, 158★
 Greenwell's Glory 106
 Grenadier Special 105, 156★
 GRHE Green Marabou 108, 152–153★
 Hawthorn Fly 160★
 Hover Fly 159★
 Jersey Herd 108, *163*
 Living Damsel 55
 Mickey Finn 61, *163*
 Minkie 125
 Missionary 108
 Muddler Minnow 125
 Olive Damsel 108, 152★
 Olive Grizzle Palmer 55, 58, 108, 156★
 Orange Fritz Booby 152★
 Partridge & Silver Nymph 105, 154–156★
 Peeping Caddis 55,
 Pheasant Tail Nymph (PTN) 55, 154★
 Red Tag Wingless Wickham's 156★
 Rough GRHE *54*, 55, *96*, 105, *145*, 153★
 Seal's Fur Emerger 158–159★
 Shuck Fly *147*, 154★
 Silver Corixa 99
 Silver Spider 58
 Terrestrial Beetle 161★
 Whiskey Fly 61, *163*
 White Marabou *163*
 Wickham's Fancy 106
 Yellow Tag GRHE 154★
 Zulu 157★
attractors 57, 61
autopsies 88–99

back-drifting 21, 140
backing 25
bank fishing 119, 128–130
barometric pressure 167–168
beetles *95*, 104–105, 110
birds 79, 181–182
blanks 7, 75–76
bloodworm *94*, 102
blue trout 56
boat fishing 130–140
boat gear 31–33
boats 130–131
boobies 123–125
braided leaders 42–43, 117
braided loop 41–42
brown trout 55, *56*, 175
buzzers 59, *92*, *96*, *101*–103, *122*

caddis 104
caenis 105–106
calm lanes 81–82, *83*
casting
 distance 34, *37*
 double haul technique 36, *37*
 faults 38–39
 overhead cast 35–36
 professional tuition 40
 roll cast 36
clothing 29
cloud cover 165–166
commandos 166
confidence 50, 112

corixa *95*, 104–*105*
cormorant *54*, 171
Cove, Arthur 146
curiosity of trout 53, 57, 61, 87, 98

daddy long legs *109*
damsels *97*, 101, *103*–104
daphnia *91*, 103
dayflies – see upwinged flies
deceivers 55–57, 59–61, 117
disabled anglers *12*, 140
'disturbed water' phenomenon 39
drifting 136–140
drifting the line 116, 119–120
drogue 32, 137–138
dry fly fishing 66–67

earthworms *93*
Elinor Trout Fishery *frontispiece*
empty fish 98
etiquette and behaviour 13, 180–181
evening rise 121, *123*, 170
exact imitation 55, 57–59
Eyebrook Reservoir *8, 15, 23*, 75, *78, 79, 166*, 174,
    178, 179, 184

fanning the casts 39, 114–116
feathers *97*
features and structure 81
feeding patterns of trout 52, 85
fishfinders 32–*33*, 79, 81
fishing clubs 78, 176
fishing diary 126–127, 188
fishing lunches – see food and drink
fishing methods 117–126
fishing season 79–80, 165, 169
flashers 57, 61, 161, *163*
flat calms 121
flies – *see* artificial flies
flies, choice of 52–61, 112–114, 149
fluorocarbon 43–*44*, 48, 51
fly boxes 27
fly dressing 11, 141–147
fly lines
    changing 22–23
    cleaning 23–24
    colour 19
    floating 19, 22, 40
    intermediate 19–21
    line twist 38–39
    marking 39
    silk 17–18
    sinking 21, 40
    twist remover 23–*24*
    ultra fast sinking 21

visibility of *18*–19
weight forward taper 16
fly reels 25–26
fly rods 14–*16*
food and drink 29–30
foul-hooked fish 76
freshwater hog louse 104–105
fry *93*, 106–108, 125–*126*

general public 176–177
genetic hackles *142*
Grafham Water *126*, 175
Greenwell, Canon 146

Herbert, Graham 6, *20*
hooks 144, 148–149
hot spots *79*, 80–81
hover fly *110*

indicators 121–123
induced take 60, 61, 66
inedible items 85
intelligence of trout 53
Ivens, T.C. 15, 189

Jones, Ifor 6

Kamasan fly hooks 51, 149
knots
    failure 47–48
    lubricating 49
    recommended 44–47
    wind 36, 50

lady anglers *13*
land bred flies – *see* terrestrials
landing nets *26*–27
large fish *15, 73, 169, 175, 178*
leader (or tippet)
    breaking strain 51
    design 62–67
    droppers 63
    length 43, 62–63
    materials 43–44
    turnover 62–63
    visibility *44*, 168–169
leech *96*
Leicestershire Fly Fishing Association (LFFA) 6,
176, *177*
life jacket 32, 132
lightning 165, 167–168
limit bags *8, 58*, 74–75, *122*
line bites 76
line tray 31
locating trout 77–85

loch style 136–139
long lining 136–137
loop to loop connection 41–42
lures 57, 61, 87, 88, 161, *163*

marrow spoon 27, 88, 89, *90*
mayflies *106, 107*
midges – see buzzers
Miller, Andy 6, 75, *78*
mirror 134
muddlers 124–125
muddy edge feeders *124*, 125

nets – *see* landing nets
netting fish *71*, 72
'Northampton' style 138–139
novices 35, 174–179, 180
nylon 43–*44*, 48, 51
nymph fishing 117, 118

olives 101, 106
outboard motors 131

patience 175–176
Pitsford Reservoir *124, 137*
playing fish *70*–72
points 118–119
polarized glasses 27, 29
polymer leaders 42–43, 117
'pull' 22, 68–69

questions 77–87

rainbow trout *55*
Ravensthorpe Reservoir *42*
recognition points 59, 148
retrieve
    methods 64–66, 114–116
    roly-poly 66
Ringstead Grange Trout Fishery 98, *113*
rise forms 86
rising fish 79, 86, 120–121
Rutland Water *56, 82, 130, 133, 173*, 175, *182*

safety 29, 32, 129, 131–133, 174–175
salmon 87
scum lanes 82, *83*
seasons 79–80, 169
seat riser block *31*, 186
secrecy 9, 81
sedges *104*
selective feeding 53, 88, *91, 95*, 109
senses of trout 52–53
Shakespeare 28–29
shooting heads 17

short lining 136
shrimps 104–105
shucks 103, 146–*147*
slack line 22, 36, *37*
smash takes *49*, 70
snails 108
spooning fish 89
sticklebacks *107*
stocking 171–172, *173*
strike 68–69
suggestive deceivers 55–57, 59–61
'suspended nymph' method 67–68

tackle bags and boxes *28–29*
'take' 68–69
tangles 36, 63
terrestrials *95*, 108–110
Thornton Reservoir *75, 140, 172, 175*
thunderstorms 165, *166*, 167–168
time of day 170
trailing 140
trolling 140
tube flies *139*
'two fish at a time' 72–74

upwinged flies 105–106

vegetable matter 88, 94, 108

waders 30–31
wading 128–130
Walker, Richard 146, 159, 189
'washing line' method 67
water
    clarity 168–169
    temperature 82–85, 98, 164–165
water bugs 104–105
'Water Shed' 157
waterproofs 29
weather 165
webbing-to-clamp device 31–32, 187
weed 81, 94, 108, 170–171
'wet and dry' methods 67–68, 121
wet fly methods 117–126
Wheelyboats 12
wildlife 181–183
wind
    direction 166–167
    speed 167
window, trout's 134–135
Wright, Mal 6, 144
wrist break 38

yawing 135–136